GOLD

HISTORICAL AND ECONOMIC ASPECTS

COLORADO MOUNTAIN COLLEGE
LRC---WEST CAMPUS
Glenwood Springs, Colo 81601

GOLD

HISTORICAL AND ECONOMIC ASPECTS

Advisory Editor
KENNETH CARPENTER

EARLY DAYS ON THE YUKON

WILLIAM OGILVIE

COLORADO MOUNTAIN COLLEGE
LRC---WEST CAMPUS
Glenwood Springs, Colo 81601

ARNO PRESS
A New York Times Company
New York • 1974

Reprint Edition 1974 by Arno Press Inc.

Reprinted from a copy in The State
Historical Society of Wisconsin Library

GOLD: Historical and Economic Aspects
ISBN for complete set: 0-405-05910-8
See last pages of this volume for titles.

Manufactured in the United States of America

Library of Congress Cataloging in Publication Data

Ogilvie, William, 1846-1912.
    Early days on the Yukon & the story of its gold finds.

      (Gold: historical and economic aspects)
    Reprint of the 1913 ed. published by J. Lane, London
and New York.
    1. Yukon Territory--History. 2. Yukon Valley--
History. 3. Klondike gold fields. I. Title.
II. Series.
F1093.O35 1974   917.19'1   74-356
ISBN 0-405-05917-5

EARLY DAYS ON THE YUKON

EARLY DAYS ON THE YUKON
& THE STORY OF ITS GOLD FINDS
BY WILLIAM OGILVIE
D.L.S., F.R.G.S. WITH 32 ILLUSTRATIONS

LONDON: JOHN LANE, THE BODLEY HEAD
NEW YORK: JOHN LANE COMPANY
TORONTO: BELL & COCKBURN: MCMXIII

WILLIAM BRENDON AND SON. LTD., PRINTERS, PLYMOUTH

TO
MY WIFE

PREFACE

AFTER many years of service in the Yukon Territory, Mr. Ogilvie acquired an intimate knowledge of its peoples, its geography, and its resources.

Accuracy was one of his salient characteristics, and by close observation, careful weighing of conflicting reports, and a retentive memory, he has endeavoured to bequeath to the public an authentic history of this Arctic region.

Much of the information contained in the *Klondike Official Guide*, published by Mr. Ogilvie in 1898, is embodied in this book, illumined by incidents and stories of camp life.

The Yukon Territory and Alaska are so bound together by a common interest that Canadians and Americans have joined hands in a combined effort toward the best development of the country.

While the International Boundary is a broad line through the wilderness, men in this land of the midnight sun are prone to forget nationality in remembering the tie of Arctic Brotherhood.

A pathfinder and explorer, undaunted by hardships and forgetful of self-interest, Mr. Ogilvie devoted the best years of his life to the Yukon Territory, and I commend to the kindly reading public, British and American, his history of the *Early Days on the Yukon.*

I gratefully acknowledge the courtesies extended to me in connection with this publication by Mr. Ogilvie's old friends and colleagues in the Dominion Government, Dr. E. Deville, Surveyor-General of Canada, Dr. W. F. King, Chief Astronomer, and Dr. Otto Klotz, Assistant Chief Astronomer.

O. P. R. OGILVIE.

CONTENTS

CHAPTER		PAGE
I.	COMPARATIVE STATEMENT OF GEOGRAPHICAL AND POLITICAL DISTINCTIONS OF AMERICAN TERRITORY OF ALASKA AND THE YUKON TERRITORY OF CANADA	3
II.	BOUNDARY MATTERS	14
III.	STORY OF ATTEMPTED CRIME AND THE SWIFT JUSTICE WHICH FOLLOWED IT	42
IV.	REMARKS ON MR. OGILVIE'S SURVEY	52
V.	TRADING AND TRADING POSTS ON THE RIVER	63
VI.	GOLD DISCOVERIES AND MINING	84
VII.	FIRST GOLD SENT OUT	105
VIII.	DISCOVERY OF THE KLONDIKE	115
IX.	MR. OGILVIE'S VISIT TO THE COUNTRY IN 1887-8 AND OBSERVATIONS MADE THEN	137
X.	WINTER WORK IN 1895-6	156
XI.	WORK DONE ON THE CREEKS BY MR. OGILVIE	177

CONTENTS

CHAPTER		PAGE
XII.	Local Excitement as Wealth of Klondike was Revealed	205
XIII.	Experiences in Camp and on River	215
XIV.	Methods of Mining	225
XV.	Administration of Law in Early Camps	245
XVI.	Reflections	267
XVII.	Social Customs	290
XVIII.	Home	297

APPENDIX

Present Conditions. By Dr. Alfred Thompson, M.P. 302

ILLUSTRATIONS

OGILVIE'S PARTY ON THE YUKON, CARRYING IN TWO YEARS' PROVISIONS, 1887	*Cover Design*
WILLIAM OGILVIE	*Frontispiece*
	FACING PAGE
UNALASKA, 1897	8
DAWSON CITY, 1897	24
141ST MERIDIAN. AUTHOR'S LOCATION 1887, AND CORRECTED LINE IN 1907	30
LOOKING UP DYEA PASS FROM TRAIL AT FIRST BRIDGE, 1887	40
BEGINNING OF CIRCLE CITY, ALASKA, 1894	66
FORTYMILE, 1895	68
CHIEF CHARLEY	72
INDIAN CAMP AT FORT SELKIRK, 1887	76
ALASKA COMMERCIAL CO.'S STEAMER "SUSIE"	82
ARTHUR HARPER, PIONEER MINER	88
FRED HART	102
ALASKA COMMERCIAL CO.'S WHARF, ST. MICHAEL, ALASKA, 1897	106
JOE LADUE'S HOUSE AT OGILVIE, 1895	120
ROBERT HENDERSON	126
NEAR THE BOUNDARY. ONE-HALF THE PREVIOUS DAY'S BAG	134
COL. S. B. STEELE, CHIEF FACTOR FOR LAW AND ORDER IN THE YUKON	150
SLUICING ON BONANZA CREEK, NO. 2 BELOW	166

ILLUSTRATIONS

	FACING PAGE
Dump on Claims 5 and 6, Eldorado	184
Northern Dog-Team	192
Klondikers Mushing over Dyea Pass, 1898	210
Bonanza Valley shortly after a Strike, 1896	226
Wind-driven Sleds on Taku River, 1895–6	240
Tagish Lake Police and Custom Station, Hon. Clifford Sifton, Major Walsh, and Inspector Strickland standing together, 1897	246
Alaska Commercial Co.'s Warehouse, Dawson, 1897	254
Ice Jam at Ogilvie Bridge, showing Guggenheim Dredge at Work	260
Dawson, 1901	266
Breaking Up the Ice on the Yukon River	272
Looking South from Point on the 141st Meridian, 1896	280
Looking up Taku Pass near Summit, 1895	288
Interior of Author's Camp near Boundary, 1895	298

EARLY DAYS ON THE YUKON

EARLY DAYS ON THE YUKON

CHAPTER I

COMPARATIVE STATEMENT OF GEOGRAPHICAL AND POLITICAL DISTINCTIONS OF AMERICAN TERRITORY OF ALASKA AND CANADIAN TERRITORY OF YUKON

THE United States territory of Alaska and the Yukon Territory of Canada are so intimately associated in the public mind that few except scholars or students think of them as separate polities, yet they are so different geographically and politically that we will, by way of introduction, make a short comparison.

Alaska is a peninsula at the extreme north-west angle of the North American Continent, and has a main coast-line of not less than six thousand miles, and that of the archipelago of islands along its western coast and the Aleutian Islands will aggregate fully half as much more. When the survey of the whole coast-line is completed it is not unlikely that a total coast-line of about twelve thousand miles will be found. About one-third of this is open to navigation the year round, the rest is closed more than half the time.

Yukon Territory has a coast-line on the Arctic Ocean of less than two hundred miles, which is closed nearly three-fourths of the year. The area of Alaska is about five hundred and ninety-one thousand square miles, that of Yukon about two hundred and seven thousand square miles; so Alaska has only about fifty square miles of territory to every mile of coast-line, while Yukon has over a thousand. The potentialities for development, therefore, are apparently vastly in favour of Alaska, but the mighty river which flows longitudinally through both, in such a way as to give each the best possible service, reduces the disproportion of coast-line against Yukon, and at present gives each nearly an equal chance.

This Yukon River is unique among rivers, in that it rises within fifteen miles of tidal waters in the Dyea Inlet on the Pacific coast, whence it flows in a north-westerly direction nearly one thousand miles, just crossing the Arctic Circle, where it turns south-west through the middle of Alaska, and then flows more than twelve hundred miles until it reaches the ocean within sight of which it rose; for we may properly call Bering Sea a part of the Pacific Ocean. This grand stream

COMPARATIVE STATEMENT

is also surprising in the length of navigation way it gives in proportion to its length, for less than fifteen miles north from where its tiniest streamlets trickle from the summit of Dyea Pass lies beautiful Lake Bennet, whose head is the beginning of steamboat navigation on this noble stream. From the starting-point of those same streamlets one can look down on other streamlets beginning their steep descent of the Dyea Pass to the waters of the wide Pacific, only as far away on the south as beautiful Bennet is on the north.

From the head of Bennet to Bering Sea is about twenty-five hundred miles by the course of the river, and all this length, with the exception of three and a half miles at the Cañon and Rapids, is navigable, thus all its length, except the first fifteen steep miles down the slope of its source and the three and a half at the Cañon, is navigable. Can this be said of any other river in the world?

From the head of Lake Bennet to the Cañon, ninety-five miles, of which sixty-four is lake and thirty-one river, steamboats ran in the first years of the Klondike excitement. The Cañon and Rapids include a fall of about thirty-five feet, but are not so dangerous as to prohibit the passage of small steamers down them, as was done with those plying above them when the railroad was completed from the head of Bennet to White Horse, just below them, which made their service no longer profitable, but it would be practically impossible to get those steamers up again. That a river so long, and flowing as it does for more than two-thirds of its length through a veritable sea of mountains, has only this slight break in continuous steamboat navigation from within a look from its head to its mouth, is indeed worthy of remark, and it may with truth be said it is a strange river in a strange land.

About one-third of the total length is in Yukon Territory, and this with its affluent streams, the Takhina, the Teslin (better known as the Hootalinqua), the Pelly, the Stewart, all navigable for greater or less distances, and all of them hundreds of miles in length, together with other streams not navigable, go to make up in Yukon nearly as much length of stream as there is in Alaska, where the affluents, though not so numerous, are, like the Tanana and Koyukuk, navigable for long distances. Altogether, this river with its tributaries gives about three thousand five hundred miles of ordinary flat-bottomed steamboat navigation, through a country so strange and magnificent that it is well worth a journey from Seattle or Vancouver to see it; a journey which takes us through the most wonderful run of inland ocean navigation in the world, where we travel for a thousand miles on oceans blue, where at only three points for a few hours at a time are we subjected to any of the discomfort of sea travel, sailing for days through inland passages whose shores are mountains with green slopes fading into everlasting whiteness, often lost in the indefinable haze of the heavens above. From Skagway one hundred and ten miles of railway through a scenic route seldom surpassed lands us at the little town of White Horse just below the rapids. From here, in the summer season, comfortable steamers take us to the world-wide known Dawson, the port for the Golden Klondike, where over a hundred millions in treasure have been unearthed, and where hundreds of millions more await the man with the machine to bring them forth. In winter a stage line carries the passenger between these points in comparative comfort, travelling only in daylight and stopping over-night at comfortable road-houses, as they are termed. The journey is made in about five days. The steamboat takes about forty-eight hours on the down, and twice that on the up, run.

From Dawson to St. Michael, the entry port for the Yukon Basin, situated on an island of the same name in Bering Sea, about seventy miles north of the mouth of the Yukon River, is about seventeen hundred miles. It is a beautiful run, at one point, Fort Yukon, just crossing the Arctic Circle, and if the passage is made early enough in the season the midnight sun may be seen. The journey is usually made in five days, but contrary or high winds at the mouth of the river may prolong it considerably more.

A comfortable run of nine hundred miles across Bering Sea brings us to the first, and generally the only, call port on the way home, Dutch Harbour, or Unalaska, within sight of each other, both on Unalaska Island, one of the Aleutian group. To the student of natural and historic subjects the stay cannot fail to be interesting. From this point a straight run of about seventeen hundred miles brings us to Seattle or Vancouver, and about two thousand and forty to San Francisco. To one with a taste for the original, the primeval, on this route he can enjoy it as nowhere else, and with all the comfort of modern travel, at moderate cost. To one who has seen the lands of legend, of medievalism, and of history, this journey will round out his education, enliven his satisfaction with all, and develop his powers of comparison. It is a journey unique, interesting, and instructive beyond description, and is well worth undertaking by any one who can afford the cost, which is quite as reasonable as that of ordinary ocean voyages.

POLITICAL DISTINCTIONS

Politically they are both territories, that is they are not yet endowed with statehood, or provincial autonomy, though Yukon is practically so. Each territory has a Governor, or as the style in Yukon is, a Commissioner, who is appointed by the Federal Government and represents the terri-

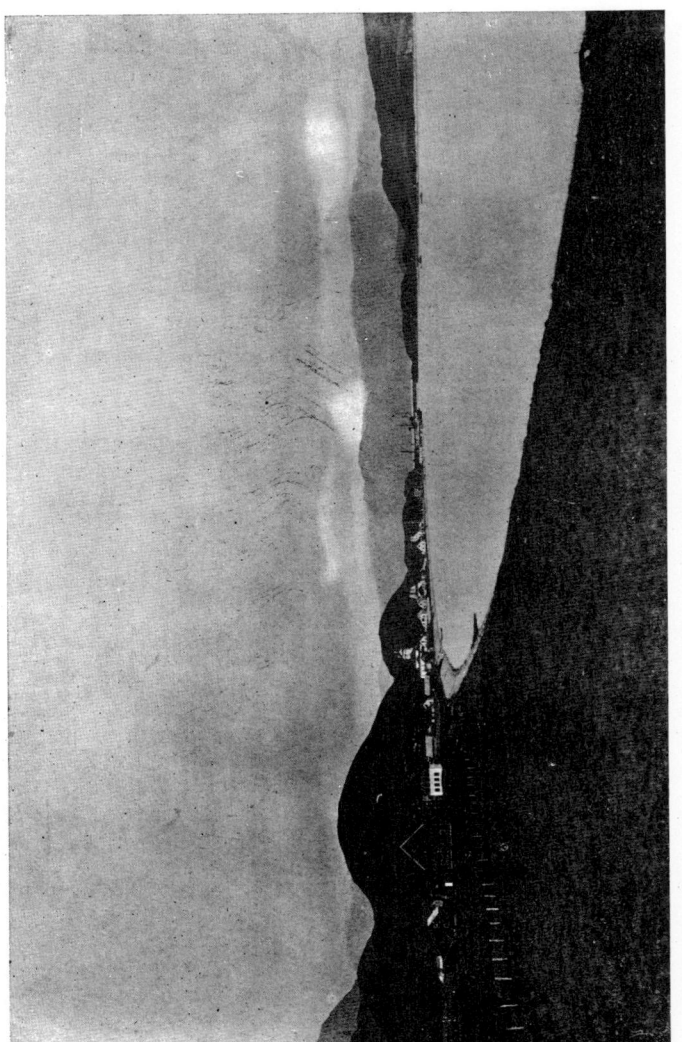

UNALASKA, 1897

torial needs to the central government. In Alaska the Governor is assisted in this service by an elected delegate to the United States House of Representatives, who may discuss but cannot vote. The Public Works of the territory are carried on by Federal officers who report direct to Washington, and look after the appropriations for their respective services.

In Yukon the Commissioner-Governor has a complete staff of officials which attends to all the public service of the territory under his direction. Though the Commissioner has no direct control over the mining regulations, they being the subject of legislation by the Federal Parliament, and adjustment and application by "Orders in Council" of the Federal Cabinet, his advice is a matter of very serious interest to the Minister of the Interior, and through him to the Government. In order that all the territory may receive its share of attention in the distribution of public expenditure, a local council of ten members is elected by the people of the territorial districts to represent them in the Council meetings, which are held once a year, in the summer. This Council elects its own speaker, and its proceedings are conducted according to the rules of parliamentary procedure; it regulates the imposition of taxes within the territory, and the machinery for their collection. The distribution of those taxes, and the appropriation from the Federal Government, is controlled by the Council, it providing its own staff of officials for that purpose, which acts under the general supervision of the Commissioner. Thus, though the territory has not a fully fledged legislature, it has what is practically the same thing. Then, too, at every Dominion General Election it elects a member of Parliament to represent it in the Federal House of Commons, who is not restricted in any of the powers or privileges of membership in that body, and this notwithstanding that the population so represented is less than one-half the quota entitling other parts of Canada to representation.

JUDICIAL FACILITIES

The territory of Alaska is attached to the Ninth Circuit Court of the United States, the judges of which constitute a Court of Appeal for the district. Two of them live in California, one in Oregon. The district, or circuit, includes Alaska, Arizona, California, Idaho, Montana, Nevada, Oregon, Washington, and Hawaii. It therefore extends from north latitude 31 degrees to 71 degrees, and from west longitude $109\frac{1}{2}$ degrees to, in the case of Hawaii, $157\frac{1}{2}$ degrees, and in the case of the most westerly of the Aleutian Islands of Alaska, which, however, are hardly worth considering in this respect, to 187 degrees west or 173 east. In area it covers 1,375,910 square miles, or more than forty-five per cent of the area of the United States without Alaska, and thirty-eight per cent of it with it. Its total population by the last census was 3,204,652, a little more than four per cent of the population of the country; whereas the average for the nine circuits would be eleven per cent.

Yukon Territory has three resident judges at a salary of ten thousand dollars per year each, and a police magistrate at a salary of six thousand seven hundred. The three judges attend to all the Superior Court business of the territory. The three shall sit in *banc* at appointed times and places, when they may hear and dispose of motions for new trials, appeals, and motions in the nature of appeals. Appeals from the judgments of the Territorial Court shall be made to the Supreme Court of Canada under certain restrictions it is needless to cite here, and from the Supreme Court of Canada appeal lies to the Judicial Committee of the House of Lords, the highest tribunal in the British Empire, also under certain restrictions. The sittings of this tribunal are attended by a representative of the Supreme Court of Canada to assist in Canadian cases. The area of the territory, as we have seen, is a little over two hundred thousand square miles, or only a little more than a seventh of that of the Ninth Circuit Court District of the United States, and the population, principally located along the

Yukon River, is not more than ten thousand, or less than the thirty-second hundredth part of that of the Ninth District.

In addition to these judicial facilities the Canadian Government keeps on duty an adequate number of its "Royal North-West Mounted Police." This force is semi-civil and semi-military in character. It is drilled as an unit of an army, but its duty is always on the frontier, and the enforcement of law and order is its especial province. Every officer is a magistrate, and every private or "constable" a policeman, so law and order march hand in hand with the force wherever it may be, and it is always where it is needed. In case of necessity it can, and does, act as a trained band of soldiers, notably so in the North-West Rebellion of 1885.

REASON FOR CONFUSION OF NAMES

Perhaps the reason for the confusion regarding the identity of these two territories is the fact that many of the earliest gold discoveries were made in the vicinity of the International Boundary Line, and their accompanying settlements and camps being largely made by citizens of the United States, there was a disposition to call all the region so occupied "Alaska," until the boundary line was marked, but the habit was formed then, though it was only two or three years after the earliest diggings. In those days, as most of the miners had to go out in the fall, and while out always referred to the region of their labours as Alaska, it came to be all so called, and the habit being thus formed, it is generally yet referred to by that title.

CHAPTER II

BOUNDARY MATTERS

IN the year 1741 a Danish navigator named Vitus Bering, who at an early age entered the service of Russia under Peter the Great, and continued in it during the reign of some of his successors, with his lieutenant, Alexis Chirikoff, each in command of a ship, fell on the islands off the west coast of the continent at two widely different points within a day of each other. They sailed from Okhotsk on the sea of that name, and all that part of the water they crossed north of the Aleutian Islands is now known as " Bering Sea." This discovery gave Russia a claim to the islands so found, and the mainland behind them. It is outside the scope of this history to deal further with Bering's work, and it is only referred to as the origin of boundary matters in this region. The sequence will appear later on.

Three-quarters of a century before this, to be exact, May, 1670, the " Hudson's Bay Company " had been chartered by Charles II of England to trade in the interior of the continent along the waters emptying into the bay from which the company took its name. Soon after the Russians fell on the west coast they began occupying points for fur-trading bases. About this time the Hudson's Bay Company, and its rival the North-West Fur Trading Company, originated in Montreal in 1783, had advanced far beyond the watershed of Hudson's Bay, the latter company having planted a post at far-away Lake Athabasca in 1786, and three years later that company's intrepid lieutenant, Alexander Mackenzie, having learned of the great river now named after him, with four Canadians and one German, in his own canoe, and two crews of natives, descended the river marked on our maps as Great Slave River, but locally known as the Peace, to Great Slave Lake, and after many discouraging delays in it, got into the river he was looking for, which he descended to the Arctic Ocean. He was at first doubtful as to what body of water he had fallen on, but the consistent rise and fall of the tide, though only about two feet, and the sight of whales convinced him he was on the ocean. He had to fight his way back by paddle more than a thousand miles from the sea to the lake, and across it one hundred and forty to Great Slave River, and up it nearly two hundred and seventy to Lake Athabasca, thence twenty or so home. The round trip is three thousand miles, and as nearly three hundred of it, back and forth, is in Great

Slave Lake, which has a total length of more than three hundred miles, with a width upwards of forty in places, it is, in the stretch he crossed, most tempestuous at times; indeed, the whole stretch of the Mackenzie is so wide and straight that an up or down wind makes it rough for small boats, and to those who have had experience in such voyages, his appears wonderful, under the circumstances. His base of supplies was the country along the river, and with the fire-arms of those days much time had to be set apart for foraging. Game no doubt was plentiful, but a straight meat diet requires a lot of it; incredible to the uninitiated is the amount a healthy specimen of the *genus homo* will consume in a day. The ordinary ration for one person in fresh moose meat used to be eight pounds, but sometimes in lieu of meat or other ration, where game was plentiful and readily accessible, a charge of powder and shot, or a bullet was substituted, if the rationee agreed. It has been said that the ammunition ration was often accepted, because it proved a source of profit, as with one such ration enough provisions for a week or more could be secured, and the saved charges could be sold at what was considered good profit, though not many now would consider it of much account. It is hardly necessary to say that bread and vegetables, the staff of life, as we in civilization know it, had practically no place in the larder there, at that time.

BOUNDARY MATTERS

While at the mouth of the river, Mackenzie learned from an Indian, who had come from a tribe farther west, of another large river flowing through the region he came from, and a trading-post on a long point running far out into a great lake which he called the "White Man's Lake." The trading-post, Mackenzie conjectured, was Unalaska, and the river he thought must be Cook's River; so little was known of the geography of the region. With his usual intrepidity he tried to persuade this Indian to guide him and his party to the new stream, but nothing would induce the Indian to go. Had Mackenzie succeeded how differently might the history of this river, which we now know as the Yukon, have been written. That it would have been so, we may rest assured, for Mackenzie let no moss grow under his feet in those northern ranges when there was anything to be gained for his company in the fur line.

Three years after the discovery and exploration of his great river, Mackenzie started—October 10th, 1792—from his inland post at Athabasca to ascend the Peace and essay a journey to the Pacific coast. Before ice began running he had reached a point about five hundred and fifty miles above the lake, about opposite to the mouth of Smoky River, where he built winter quarters and remained till spring, hunting, trapping, and trading with the natives, preparing food and clothing, and building a special canoe for use on his journey to the Pacific in the following summer. When I first visited the Peace valley in 1883, the remains of his buildings could in part be seen. Three or four years after that date the Rev. John Gough Brick, an Anglican missionary who had been stationed at Dunvegan, some fifty miles farther up the river, moved down to this spot, where he established a mission, and a farm, on which he raised magnificent wheat and vegetables. In conjunction with the farm he attempted an industrial school for the Indians. Soon after his removal the Roman Catholic Mission at Dunvegan, in charge of the Rev. F. A. Husson, also established a mission, school, and farm near Mr. Brick's. This laid the foundation for a flourishing settlement, where wheat of the finest quality, and vegetables equally good, have been grown for a generation. Mackenzie was not a prophet nor the son of one, and had no visions except those connected with the fur trade, but could he have looked ahead and seen but a glimpse of the possibilities of the country he was leading the way to, in another, vaster, and more permanent field, what a different impression he might have conveyed to the world of the region of his arduous labour.

His journey to the coast was continued in the spring of 1793, after dispatching six canoes loaded with the furs he had collected during the winter to Chippewyan.

The journey to the ocean was continued in spite of hardship, difficulty, and danger of more than the ordinary grade even in that day and region. On the 22nd of July the goal was reached, and he painted on a rock the simple announcement: " Alexander Mackenzie from Canada by land the 22nd of July, one thousand seven hundred and ninety-three." This journey could not be less than twelve hundred miles each way, and to accomplish such a feat at the date he did, and in the time and place he did, eclipses many of the much-vaunted journeys of more recent date. His motive in part appears to have been to discover the river he had learned of near the mouth of the Mackenzie, but as we now know, he was far south of any of its tributaries. His assumption was natural enough, seeing that the tributaries of the Mackenzie headed, some of them, much farther south than he was.

In 1821 these rival companies were merged, retaining the name of the old company, in the " Hudson's Bay Company." This tended to arrest the vigour with which trading-posts were pushed into the wilderness, for competition ceased. This, while not connected with the boundary question, may have indirectly affected it, for if the North-West Company had kept on advancing as energetically after that date as it did before, assuming it still in existence, it would likely have had posts on the Porcupine and

Yukon in a very few years, and the boundary negotiators between England and Russia might have had to consider posts in the interior, and provide for them in the determination of the position of the boundary line across the peninsula from the Pacific to the Arctic. As it proved, if the British did nothing in the way of exploring and exploiting the Porcupine and Yukon region in the first three decades of the last century, neither did the Russians. It was not till 1830 that a Russian armed brig, under the command of Midshipman Etolin, was directed to examine Norton Sound and report on its facilities for trade. The following year Baron Wrangell dispatched Lieutenant Tebenkof to establish a station and settlement on St. Michael Island. In 1832-3 a Russian half-breed explored the delta of the Yukon, and the Anvik River tributary to it, and in 1838 an employee of the Russian-American Company named Malakof ascended the Yukon in the native skin boats (bidarras) as far as Nulato, about five hundred and seventy-five miles from the sea. He built a post here, but as he had only two men with him, and the natives were not too friendly, he returned in the fall. Nothing more was done till 1842, when Lieutenant Zagoskin, of the Russian Navy, went up and rebuilt the post, which has been maintained since. This appears to be as far up-stream as the Russians ventured with settlement, though they made regular boat trips farther up in quest of furs. The fur trade was the only question with these pioneers: geography, meteorology, history, and all other matters of importance and interest to the student were practically ignored, and we can learn little or nothing from such records as were kept, except what concerned the fur trade.

Before leaving this post we may refer to a tragedy that occurred in 1851, which being associated with another great tragedy is of interest. Some time previous to this date rumours had reached the British Government that some white men were seen by Indians wandering in a destitute state, near a lake north of this point. Ever on the alert for tidings of the ill-fated Sir John Franklin Expedition, whose end had not yet been settled, the British Admiralty sent Lieutenant Barnard, of the warship *Enterprise*, to learn what he could about this rumour. He was compelled to winter there. The Russian agent in charge of the post was, for reasons sufficient to the natives in the district, not popular, and during the stay of Barnard some of the more aggressive of them decided to kill the agent. The stranger they knew nothing about, but as he was there, and white, he had to go too. They were attacked, the Indians afterwards reported, in the early hours of the morning. The agent, it was said by them, hid his head in the bedding, but the Lieutenant jumped up and seized a musket he had, with which he kept them at bay till he was disembowelled by one who came in on him, crawling along the floor. The remains of both were afterwards buried on a knoll by the river bank a short distance below the post. On my way down the stream in 1897 I visited the graves, and saw at the head of Barnard's a neat board painted white, on which, in black letters, was a succinct account of the tragedy in Latin, the whole being the work of the Rev. Father Barnum, a Jesuit missionary. He is a nephew of the celebrated P. T. Barnum, the great showman.

ADVANCES BY THE HUDSON'S BAY COMPANY

A few years after the amalgamation of the two companies, George Simpson (afterward Sir George) made a canoe voyage across the continent from Montreal in the east to the Pacific coast, following pretty closely the routes already traversed by his predecessors in the region. The report of his journey, and account of the resources and facilities he learned of, largely shaped adventure in the Wild West; for though business was the main factor in every progressive step, adventure, under the circumstances, was unavoidable.

A decade or so after the Simpson journey, outposts began to be pushed farther and farther west and north, and about the time Zagoskin was re-establishing Nulato, we find a clerk in the

BOUNDARY MATTERS

service of the company, named Robert Campbell, making his way from the head-waters of the Liard, a tributary of the Mackenzie, to the headwaters of the Yukon on a stream which he called the Pelly, after the then Governor, or President, of his company. In the year 1843, accompanied by two French-Canadians, a half-breed interpreter, and three Indians, he essayed descent of the new-found stream, and finding nothing too formidable for the safe passage of their birch bark canoe, he continued to the junction with another stream, which he called the Lewes, after a fellow employee. The Indians he met so far were civil, but as he had journeyed more than five hundred miles from his base in a fragile canoe, and his source of supplies was the forest, and his weapons the slow flintlocks of the time, he did not think it advisable to continue farther, so returned, in which movement he was hurried by the very suspicious actions of the Indians, as related by him in a brochure on the expedition some time afterwards. From the junction of the streams he then discovered, he called the united waters the Pelly. It is hardly necessary to say that the river he named the Lewes, and the part of the Pelly below the confluence, is all now known as the Yukon, being on the steamboat route from White Horse to Dawson, and it would be inconvenient to call parts of the same stream by different names. Four years after, this clerk had so rushed matters that he was able to establish a trading-post at the point of confluence he had discovered. Four years after may sound to the ordinary reader like sarcasm, but it is not. When we reflect that in those days railroads were hardly known on the continent, and that the outfits for these distant posts were two and three years en route, and the returns as long getting back, we can, even at this distant day, form some idea of the enterprise necessary to originate the idea, organize the transport, and establish the post in a hitherto unknown place nearly five thousand miles from Montreal, the entry port, from where every pound of material had to be paddled in canoes on the lakes and rivers, conveyed on very primitive carts over the wide prairies, and carried on the backs of the boat's crew over the transfers from one stream or lake to another, or from one stretch of navigable water to another.

In the same year another clerk in the same company established another trading-post on the same river at a point four hundred and eighty miles farther down, where the Porcupine joins the Yukon. The builder of this post was A. H. Murray. In 1852 the coast Indians at Chilcat and Chilcoot, who found their profits from the fur trade with the interior, or " Stick Indian " as he was known, because he came from the land of forest, or " sticks," diminishing in an unaccountable way, undertook a journey to the interior to

DAWSON CITY, 1897

BOUNDARY MATTERS

investigate, and learn, if they could, who was disturbing the monopoly they had hitherto enjoyed, for they largely took from the poor Stick whatever he had, and gave him whatever they saw fit. They found Campbell the disturber of business equilibrium in his post at Selkirk and understood how the balance of trade was disturbed. To restore the balance, as they were ignorant of modern business methods, and knew only

> "The good old rule
> Sufficeth them, the simple plan,
> That they shall take who have the power
> And they shall keep who can,"

they took possession of the post, and its appurtenances, contents, hereditaments, and all other things thereto appertaining, for their sole and only use for ever, and sent Campbell and his help down-river. Campbell had gone downstream two years before to decide whether or not a post he had heard of from the Indians was the company's post at Porcupine, or Fort Yukon as it was called, and it was only then it was certainly known what the course of the great river from the mouth of the Pelly down, was. He left Selkirk this last time about the middle of August, and reached Fort Simpson on the Mackenzie by the close of navigation—about the end of September. The distance travelled is seventeen hundred miles, all of it covered by foot and small boat. He left Simpson in November by dog-team and snowshoe for St. Paul, Minnesota, twenty-five hundred miles away, and was in London, England, in March trying to induce his directorate to reestablish his post at Selkirk. In this he failed. Fort Yukon was occupied till the company was notified by Capt. C. W. Raymond of the United States Corps of Engineers in August, 1869, that the post was in American territory. As soon as practicable after this notice the post was moved up the Porcupine River far enough, it was thought, to place it in British territory, but owing to some mistake somewhere it was not moved far enough, and when the position of the International Boundary Line was approximately determined on the Porcupine in 1889, it was found to be still in American territory; following which it was abandoned, and the Hudson's Bay Company withdrew altogether from the Yukon valley.

BOUNDARY NEGOTIATIONS AND MATTER RELATED TO THEM

The boundary negotiations between Britain and Russia in 1823-4-5 were the direct outcome of an Imperial order by the Emperor of Russia, which assumed control of Bering Sea. It took direction of all shipping in that sea, and imposed regulations for its government, as much as it could if the shipping had been in a Russian port, and applied it to the shipping of all nations. The United

BOUNDARY MATTERS

States and Britain promptly protested against the closing of such a large body of water, ocean it might be termed, against their shipping. As the United States was interested only in the assumed sovereignty by Russia over what had been used as an open sea by its sailors and ships, the question between these powers was soon settled by the withdrawal of the Russian claim of exclusive control of that body of water. The adjustment with Britain, however, was not so simple, for the question of territory was pertinent, and in order to lessen to Russia the mortification of receding on the main question, the discussion of limits was associated with the maritime dispute. Through lack of exact knowledge, and more through conflicting views as to territorial rights, the negotiations dragged over two years and were once or twice on the point of being broken off altogether. In the end, however, the friendship then subsisting between the two Governments prevailed, and a treaty covering the dispute regarding the sovereignty of Bering Sea, which Russia relinquished, and delimiting the boundary line between the territories of the High Contracting Parties, as they are styled in the treaty, was ratified. In addition to relinquishing the sovereignty of Bering Sea, Russia agreed that for the term of ten years the ships of Britain would have the same rights to " frequent without any hindrance whatever, all the inland Seas, the Gulfs, Havens, and Creeks on the Coast mentioned in Article III, for the purpose of fishing, and trading with the Natives." Article III will be quoted in full further on. If any other power secured from Russia the same privilege for a longer term, Britain was to enjoy it for the same time. It was also provided that British subjects " from whatever quarter they may arrive, whether from the ocean, or the interior of the Continent," shall have the right for ever to navigate without hindrance of any kind all the streams and rivers which in their course to the Pacific Ocean may cross the line of demarcation upon the line of coast described in Article III of the treaty. In the negotiations between Britain and the United States in 1871, leading to the treaty of that year, the United States contended for the free navigation of the lower St. Lawrence River, on the ground that as it had its origin in American territory, its whole length should be free to the navigation of the country giving it birth. This was agreed to, and at the instigation of Donald A. Smith, now Lord Strathcona and Mount Royal, Canada, through her representative in the negotiations, Sir John A. Macdonald, successfully stipulated for the same rights for Canada on the Stikine, the Porcupine, and the Yukon rivers, though the right to navigate the Stikine was provided for, as we have seen, in the treaty with Russia. The concession by the United States on the other two was unavoidable in view of their contention regarding the St. Lawrence, for the cases are identical in principle.

The wording of Article III of the treaty, which defines the boundary line, is in part so vague that though Britain and Russia never had any contention over it, it was because it never came pertinently before either Government. One can be pardoned for regretting that no concrete case of dispute as to the meaning of Article III, in the minds of the negotiators, ever came up while the territory was in the possession of Russia and the parties who framed the treaty were still alive. There was ample time for this, as Russia held it forty-two years after the treaty was signed. It would have relieved us of a rather unpleasant situation, for there was not the importance attached to the region before the cession to the United States that has been since, and doubtless a settlement would have been arrived at then, sooner than since, more especially if the question had come up before the Crimean War.

The best way to show the lack of definiteness in the wording of Article III is to quote the English translation. The original treaty was written in French, the language of diplomacy of the time, and as none of the parties to it were French, I have heard it remarked by a Frenchman, who knew something of boundary matters, that it was not very good French for the purpose ; in that, however, I do not pose as a judge, and as this is not intended as a history of, nor a discussion of, the boundary question, I will simply quote Article III, in English, leaving it to those further interested to secure the French version as they may.

" III. The line of demarcation between the Possessions of the High Contracting Parties, upon the Coast of the Continent, and the Islands of America to the North-West, shall be drawn in the following manner :—Commencing from the Southernmost point of the Island called *Prince of Wales Island*, which point lies in the parallel of 54 degrees 40 minutes North Latitude, and between the 131st and 133rd degree of West Longitude (Meridian of Greenwich), the said line shall ascend to the North along the Channel called Portland Channel, as far as the point of the Continent where it strikes the 56th degree of North Latitude ; from this last-mentioned point the line of demarcation shall follow the summit of the mountains situated parallel to the Coast, as far as the point of intersection of the 141st degree of West Longitude (of the same Meridian) ; and finally, from the said point of intersection, the said Meridian Line of the 141st degree, in its prolongation as far as the Frozen Ocean, shall form the limit between the Russian and British Possessions on the Continent of America to the North-West."

The reader will notice the lack of perspicuity

141ST MERIDIAN. AUTHOR'S LOCATION 1887, AND CORRECTED LINE IN 1907

BOUNDARY MATTERS

in this Article both with regard to the term, "parallel to the Coast," and the term, "Frozen Ocean"; Arctic Ocean would have been quite as euphonic, and more specific, unless the intention was to carry the line beyond the land as far as the perpetual ice, which, in view of Britain's protest against the sovereignty of Bering Sea, is hardly probable, and it could not be expected to carry the line as far as any possible islands to be discovered in the far north. Parallel to the coast, in the case of a mountain range, if the word parallel is to be taken in its literal sense, might be said to be an impossibility, for nowhere on the surface of the globe can be found a mountain range along a coast-line parallel to it in the strict, or geometrical, sense of the word, and if it was not intended in that sense, there is room for confusion and disagreement, just as was found in this case. It seems to one from the to-day point of view that it might have, even then, been made more specific.

Though the summit of the mountains was made the boundary of the coast strip, there appeared to have been some uncertainty about it, either as to continuity, or position, or both, and it was provided in Article IV as follows :—" With reference to the line of demarcation laid down in the preceding Article it is understood :

" 1st. That the island called Prince of Wales Island shall belong wholly to Russia.

" 2nd. That whenever the summit of the mountains which extend in a direction parallel to the Coast, from the 56th degree of North Latitude to the point of intersection of the 141st degree of West Longitude shall prove to be at a distance of more than ten marine leagues from the Ocean, the limit between the British Possessions and the line of Coast which is to belong to Russia, as above mentioned, shall be formed by a line parallel to the windings of the Coast, and which shall never exceed the distance of ten marine leagues therefrom."

Ten marine leagues are equivalent, practically, to thirty-four and a half English miles.

In the recent settlement of the boundary question between Canada and the United States, the difference of view arose from these separate provisions for the location of the line. The United States contended that Article III contemplated a well-defined, continuous mountain range parallel to the coast, as was erroneously laid down on some of the earlier charts, and as no such range was found, that the provisions of Article IV should govern. Canada contended that the idea in the mind of the framers of the treaty was the summit of the peaks as seen from the ocean, which would seem to have support from the fact that before the delimitation, such as it was, was arrived at, it was proposed by Britain that the *base* of the mountains parallel to the coast should form the boundary line, to which Russia objected because the base of the mountains might in parts come down to tidal water, and she would have no territory at all at such places, so to allow Russia her strip of coast, the summit was substituted. Canada also contended that under the provisions of International Law, inlets of less than six miles in width should be considered territorial waters, and the International Boundary should cross such from peak to peak. On a chart issued by the United States in 1895 this principle was apparently recognized, but it was disclaimed as unofficial. Had the Canadian contention been accepted Canada would have secured about seventy miles of the length of Lynn Canal, and the ocean port at its head, Skagway. With a joint Commission of six members, three of them British and three American, holding such divergent views, it could not be expected that either side would have entirely its own way, to hold out for it would create a deadlock, and no result at all would be attained. It is not necessary to refer to the result here, it is so well known, as it was not received by Canada with too much satisfaction, yet it was more of a compromise than many who understood the situation expected. Canada did not secure a seaport, but on the other hand the United States did not secure the ten-marine-league limit all along the coast strip, though perhaps the strip it did get would average that on the whole. There are points where such a width would have been of advantage to it, yet it was not pressed, such, for instance, as on the Stikine River, where it is only about twenty miles from the coast in an air line, and about twenty-five by the river. Other points might be specified, but without a map of fair scale the information would have little meaning. On the whole it is doubtless better that it was settled when it was, in the way it was; delay could hardly avoid friction, and to think of war between the two branches of the English-speaking race is, all good men hope, long out of date.

EARLY ATTEMPTS AT DETERMINING THE BOUNDARY LINE

The first attempt to define the boundary line at any point, directly or indirectly, since the United States purchased Alaska, and assumed it with all the obligations of the Anglo-Russian Treaty of 1825, and there does not appear to have been any made before, was made by Capt. C. W. Raymond of the United States Corps of Engineers, who notified, as we have stated, the Hudson's Bay employees at Fort Yukon that they were in American territory. He reached the post in August, 1869, and spent some time there taking observations, astronomical, and scientific generally. He does not appear to have gone any farther up the river, and as he came up-stream on the small steamer then plying on it he returned by the same means. His work cannot properly be called an attempt to fix the boundary, as he was not near that line, but as he gave the Hudson's Bay Company people the distance they would have to go up the Porcupine to reach it, indirectly it may be called fixing the boundary.

Next in order of time, in 1877, Mr. Joseph Hunter, a civil engineer of Victoria, B.C., was delegated by the Canadian Government to make a partial survey of the Stikine River, and mark on it the boundary line. The line fixed by the Joint Commissioners, October 20th, 1903, is not far from his determination, and the difference is in favour of Canada.

Six years later Lieutenant Schwatka of the United States cavalry went over the Dyea (then spelt Taiya) Pass, and descended the Yukon from its head to its mouth. He built a large raft on the upper end of Lake Bennet, on which he and his party went down-stream as far as Tanana, thirteen hundred miles, where he procured one of the large skin boats of the country in which to continue to St. Michael. The object of his expedition was to make a census of the Indians along the river for military information. He named every feature of interest as he went along, and except where places and things had been named before, and the names well fixed, his are now generally used.

He kept notes of the courses of the river, the

rate of current, and the time taken to sail or float over them as he went along to determine roughly the position of the 141st Meridian—the International Boundary Line—but his location was a good deal out, as we might reasonably expect from the character of his survey. His line was placed a little below where the United States Military Post, Fort Egbert, now is, which is twelve miles below the true boundary.

Next was the expedition headed by the writer in 1887 for the purpose of making as definite a location as possible of the 141st Meridian on the Yukon River. This was the first direct attempt to fix with any degree of precision the boundary line, and an extended reference to it, and detailed account of the methods pursued, will, I know, be pardoned. At that time the only reliable knowledge of the upper reaches of the Yukon available were the reports and maps by Schwatka of his expedition, but as that was four years past, it was hardly reliable concerning the sentiments of the Indians along the coast towards white men entering their country, and as some unfavourable reports on their attitude had reached us from later sources, it was not altogether with feelings of pleasure the expedition left Victoria, British Columbia, May 13th of that year. Only one thing seemed to be certain, which was that there appeared to be no certainty about anything up there, and about as much reliability could be placed on any one report as on any other. There was a good deal of interest shown in the expedition, and every one had his, or her, own story of the risks about to be incurred, and how to avoid them. Under these conditions it *is easy to get information.* The voyage was made on the sidewheel steamer *Ancon*, with vertical cylinder, and walking beam engine to drive the wheels, Capt. Hunter in command. At that time only monthly voyages were made, and as a consequence the boat was loaded to the gunwales with mining and fishing appliances and needs. This steamer never was fast, and loaded as she was, she excelled herself in slowness on this voyage. Through conditions for which the ship was in no way responsible, it was May 24th when we reached Haines Mission, at the head of Chilkoot Inlet, where now stands the United States Military Post, "Fort William Henry Seward." At 11 a.m. of that day the boat left us on the threshold of our exile, for it proved that for fourteen months from that date we heard no news from any person or place, except the news of the district around us. As the steamer blew us a farewell, and dipped her flag to us, there was a lump in my throat I could not swallow, and a moisture in my eye that would not dry as long as she was in sight. Not the least of my unpleasant reflections were caused by a very disturbing report spread by a man who had passed the Mission the afternoon before. He averred he had just come from the mining camp on Stewart River, the only one then in the country, fleeing for his life, with which he wonderfully escaped. Put shortly, his startling account was that the Indians had risen against the whites and stormed the mining settlement at the mouth of the river, where was stationed for the winter nearly all the white men in the territory. A few small camps were scattered along the river, and after the storming of the post at the mouth, these were taken in detail and wiped out. He could not, or did not, tell if all except himself were killed, but his story was startling enough without that. To make it more alarming still, he told his listeners that a large band of the natives had come up the Yukon to the Cañon, where they were ambushed, awaiting the coming of the whites, whom they would exterminate as they had done those on Stewart River. If this were true, there was small chance of any escaping, for the Cañon is an ideal place for such a purpose. This part of his narrative was the most alarming to me, for if true, judging from the descriptions of the place I had heard and read, our escape, if we escaped at all, would be miraculous. To say that I heard this report, detailed as it was, and looked calmly on carrying out the programme entrusted to me is to deny my humanity, but to have turned back because of such an unconfirmed rumour would have subscribed me faithless to my trust. After considering the report and analysing it in the light of my experience with, and knowledge of, the Indian nature, I could not help feeling that there was considerable doubt about the story; for several reasons, the principal one was that Indians seldom, if ever, charged against defended positions, as was alleged in this case. Unless the Indians in that region were vastly different from others, and I had no reason to think they were, they would not storm a village of houses, the occupants armed with modern weapons while they mostly had only old-fashioned arms; anyway, storming is not their style of warfare. Then, too, it was most unlikely they would march up the river on the ice hundreds of miles from their families to ambush strangers at the Cañon, of which, probably, most of them had never heard. However, there was only one way to solve the question, go and see, and we set about getting our seven tons of impedimenta from Haines Mission to the head of Dyea Inlet, sixteen miles, and from there to the head of Lake Bennet. There were 138 souls all told of the Indian population at Dyea, two white men, and one white woman. Of the whites two were Mr. and Mrs. J. J. Healy. Mr. Healy, or, as he was better known, Capt. Healy, died at Los Angeles in the winter of 1909; his wife is still living in Southern California. The other white man was George Dickson. Both he and Healy were engaged in the Indian trade, and supplying miners entering the country. They had a good deal of influence with the coast natives, and both were helpful to me in making my arrangements for carrying our outfit to Lake Lyndeman, twenty-three miles.

The United States gunboat *Pinta* came up a few days after I did, and her presence, and the support of her commander, Capt. Newell, helped me in coming to terms with the Indians, nearly all of whom were required to get my one hundred and twenty packs over the pass.

Owing to very unfavourable weather and other adverse conditions, it was the end of June before all my stuff was laid on the beach at Bennet Lake, and the 11th of July before we found, whip-sawed lumber enough for and finished our large boat, in which all my outfit had to be taken down-river to the boundary line. Every spring the miners entering the country had to find suitable and sufficient lumber for their boats, and at that latitude and elevation the supply originally was limited, and nearly exhausted now. At first they often used rafts, but all the suitable lumber was long gone.

"While at Juneau I heard reports of a low pass from the head of Chilkoot Inlet to the head-waters of Lewes River. During the time I was at the head of Dyea Inlet I made inquiries regarding it, and found that there was such a pass, but could learn nothing definite about it from either whites or Indians. As Capt. Moore, who accompanied me, was very anxious to go through it, and as the reports of the Dyea Pass indicated that no wagon

LOOKING UP DYEA PASS FROM TRAIL AT FIRST BRIDGE, 1887

road or railroad could ever be built through it, while the new pass appeared, from what little knowledge I could get of it, to be much lower and possibly feasible for a wagon road, I determined to send the Captain by that way, if I could get an Indian to accompany him. This, I found, would be difficult to do. None of the Chilkoots appeared to know anything of the pass, and I concluded that they wished to keep its existence and condition a secret. The Tagish, or Stick Indians, as the interior Indians are locally called, are afraid to do anything in opposition to the wishes of the Chilkoots, so it was difficult to get any of them to join Capt. Moore; but after much talk and encouragement from the whites around, one of them named 'Jim' was induced to go. He had been through this pass before, and proved reliable and useful. The information obtained from Capt. Moore's exploration I have incorporated in my plan of the survey from Dyea Inlet, but it is not as complete as I would have liked. I have named this pass 'White Pass,' in honour of the late Hon. Thos. White, Minister of the Interior, under whose authority the expedition was organised. Commencing at Dyea Inlet, about two miles south of its north end, it follows up the valley of the Skaguay River to its source, and thence down the valley of another river, which Capt. Moore reported to empty into the Takone or Windy Arm of Tagish Lake. Dr. Dawson says this stream empties into the eastern arm of the Tagish Lake, and in that event Capt. Moore is mistaken. Capt. Moore did not go all the way through to the lake, but assumed from reports he heard from the miners and others that the stream flowed into Windy Arm, and this also was the idea of the Indian 'Jim' from what I could gather from his remarks in broken English and Chinook. Capt. Moore estimates the distance from tide water to the summit at about 18 miles, and from the summit to the lake at about 22 to 23 miles. He reports the pass as thickly timbered all the way through."*

* From *Ogilvie's Klondike Official Guide, 1898.*

CHAPTER III

STORY OF ATTEMPTED CRIME, AND THE SWIFT JUSTICE WHICH FOLLOWED IT

IT will fit as well here as elsewhere in this narrative to clear away the mystery associated with the story of the Indian rising at Stewart River. It is worth its space, as it shows us something of the sentiments and methods of frontier life and justice. It is also a sample of the " lost mine story," of which there are so many told.

A person whom we will designate " the Discoverer" had been in Seattle for some months during the winter of 1885–6, where he met many sojourners, for the idle months, from the Yukon ; now whether by putting together parts of separate accounts by different miners or whether, as he alleged, he got the story from one man, will never be known, but he had a story of a wonderfully rich mine, the description of which and the adjacent country he knew, and told very glibly to all who would listen. It is often difficult to catch old miners with such bait, but some will bite. By telling his story to individuals, not crowds, and giving very detailed descriptions of the river and mountains adjacent to it, he finally convinced four men, with means enough to outfit a party, that there was something substantial in what he said, and it was arranged to start for the north as soon as the season would permit, and work the wonderfully rich mine of which the Discoverer alone knew the ultimate secret. The four were to provide all the necessary outfit, and all five were to share and share alike in the clean-up. The little party left Seattle in high hopes of speedy and great wealth, toiled over the weary Dyea Pass carrying all their outfit on their backs, by relaying the distance, built their own boats at the head of Lake Bennet, and in due time reached the Stewart, up which they went in search of the hidden treasure. Arrived at the distance it was thought to be up that stream, the bends in the river, shape and size of the islands, the configuration of the mountains, and every other indication stated or hinted at by Discoverer, were observed, and examination made in the vicinity of any feature found resembling the description furnished; but no gold rewarded the search, at least not in the quantity looked for. Other groups of miners were found working on the bars and in the banks taking out good pay, but our party was not after pay, it was after a find, a fortune such as falls to the lot of but few, but it was careful to keep the prospect to itself and allay the curiosity of the old-timers by saying it would take a good look around before settling down to work, and it did. The season was almost passed when it occurred to the party that something would have to be done to supplement the supplies it brought with it, or it would run short before the next importation the following summer, everything then coming up the river, and the season being too far gone to think of going out. The party was perforce, therefore, compelled to select a place, settle down, and go to work to get out the all-requisite grub stake of the country, about four hundred and fifty dollars per man. In this it satisfactorily succeeded, when running ice put a stop to further mining operations. Winter quarters had now to be prepared, and when that was done, and the winter quiet of the region at that time took possession of them, the mischief latent in idleness began to show itself. In a party of only five there are just as likely to be five different characters as with any other number, and so it proved in this instance. Of the five only one had ever sought for gold, and their disappointment went harder with them than it would have with seasoned miners. One of the party was a very large man, and him we shall know as "the Giant." He was of a querulous disposition, and resented the trick he thought was played on them by Discoverer. Being away from all restraint, as he thought from law, Giant talked freely of what he considered ought to be done to Discoverer, for the crime he had committed in deceiving them as he had, for though they were hopeful of finding what he described to them so circumstantially, and laboured hard in search of it, it was now only too apparent to them that either Discoverer himself had been hoaxed, or he had deliberately hoaxed them, for nowhere on the river, as far as they went up, was anything at all resembling what he described found, and they went much farther up than the distance he gave them in Seattle. All the four contributors were dissatisfied with the result of their expedition. What Discoverer thought he kept to himself, and it certainly could not have been any gratification to him to hear himself and his motives discussed as they were by the others in the party; but in the case of Giant it went beyond discussion, and as the winter ennui wore on them, it became threatening, from degree to degree, till lynching was talked of. All did not approve of this, but as they never dreamed of any ill consequences from it they said nothing in objection, considering Giant only a big dissatisfied boy who must do a certain amount of blowing off, and that Discoverer deserved a scaring at least. Discoverer, however, was of a highly nervous, imaginative temperament, and as the dreary winter nights wore on him, he began to see an untimely death awaiting him in the not distant future. The frequent allusions made to his conduct, and the highly condemnatory terms used regarding it, together with the threats made by Giant, so worked on Discoverer that he decided in self-defence to kill all the others: there was no middle course as it presented itself to him. A rule of the camp was that each member should take turns of a week in cooking. Now one of the items in their outfit was a quantity of arsenic, taken along for the purpose of poisoning wild animals. This was kept in a small bottle, which was buried in the snow outside the cabin so that no risk might be run of mistaking it for something else. The week of Discoverer's turn to cook came, and ill-fortune favoured his scheme one day when all the others went out to try and secure some fresh meat. He was expected to have a hearty supper for them when they returned, and he had more than they wanted, very nearly all they ever would *want*. A staple article of food in those northern climes, and a very necessary one, is beans, and plenty of them. They are generally boiled till soft and then fried in bacon grease, and thus cooked they are both palatable, nourishing and invigorating, as the miners say, " they stick to you." Discoverer had a plentiful portion of beans for the four tired, hungry men on their return, apparently nicely done, " done to a turn," as they say there, but instead of using salt to season them with he dug up the arsenic and seasoned them with that. He

STORY OF ATTEMPTED CRIME 47

had no idea of the size of a fatal dose of the poison, and to be sure about it, used plenty. The men noticed a very unpleasant taste to the beans, and asked how it came. He replied that he had forgotten to mention that while cooking he had spilt nearly all the salt they had on top of the red-hot stove, and before he could save any of it, it was badly burned, and as he thought its strength would be reduced by the burning he had used a lot of it in the beans, and that he did not taste it so much while it was warm as now when the mess was cool. In that region in the winter, after a brisk outdoor walk, one's appetite is almost equal even to arsenic, and while they condemned the taste in auroral language, they partook of it heartily, which was their salvation, for it acted as an emetic, and their stomachs rejected the mess shortly after dining. Discoverer pleaded illness, and told them he had eaten all he wanted shortly before they came in, but for company's sake took a bite or two with them. He, too, feigned to be very sick when they were, and vomited as they did. That night all in camp were apparently near death, and their pains were excruciating. In the morning they felt somewhat better, still not well enough to take any interest in speculating on the cause of their sickness. Their sufferings were lessened a good deal by evening, when one of them became suspicious of the actions of Discoverer. It appeared to him that Discoverer's sickness was simulated, and he determined to watch him closely. As the night wore on, their pains lessened so much that all apparently fell into a sound slumber, and the watcher's efforts to keep from sleeping were heroic. As midnight approached he thought he noticed signs of attention by Discoverer, certainly he noticed that his moans lessened. At last, when apparently all were in a deep sleep, the watcher simulating his, he saw in the feeble light from the open fireplace, now flickering low, Discoverer sit up in his bunk, which was in the opposite corner of the cabin, and listen. Being at last satisfied that all were in a deep slumber he stealthily arose, tiptoed to the corner where a loaded Winchester rifle was standing, took it up, and was in the act of cocking and presenting it at one of the sleepers, when the watcher, with a shout and a spring, was on him. The trigger was pulled, but the aim was wild, and before another shot could be fired he was overpowered by the surprised slumberers and watcher. He was bound up, and after hearing the watcher's story of his suspicions and actions, they were convinced that the burned salt story was an invention. In the morning search was made for the bottle of arsenic; it was found, but the contents were materially reduced in bulk. After discussion it was decided that they would not punish him themselves, but leave it to the whole camp at the mouth of the river, so as soon as they were well enough all started for the main camp, about sixty miles away. Arrived there, in accordance with the unwritten law of mining camps, a meeting of the whole camp was convened to hear the statements of the parties to the action, and decide what punishment should be meted to the culprit. The miners told the story of the pretended secret knowledge of the lost mine, how they had organized to search for it, how they had come into the country, hunted up and down the river, under the direction of Discoverer, and found nothing resembling his description. Then how they had camped and arranged their domestic economy for the winter, concluding with the account of the almost terrible tragedy. Discoverer then told his side of it, how he had acted in good faith throughout, having got his story from one who assured him of its truth and accuracy, and he could not know that it was otherwise, till after he had learned as the others had. That instead of accepting his explanations, they were scouted with scorn and derision; he told of the threats of lynching, which were repeated so often and so earnestly, without protest from any member of the party, that he was convinced it was his life or theirs, and in that firm belief he had only done what any of them would have done—tried to save his own life. His excited, earnest manner convinced his hearers that he had only acted according to natural law. Some of his party acknowledged the truthfulness of his evidence, and admitted he had cause, from the threats that were made, for apprehension at least, and that they themselves in his position would have felt alarmed; further, they admitted that they regretted Giant was not called down in time to prevent any uneasiness, but they never dreamed that as long as there was no concerted action that Discoverer would pay any attention to threats. It appeared to the majority that Discoverer acted in self-defence only, nevertheless, he was considered an undesirable citizen, and after much discussion it was decided to banish him, so he was furnished with a sled, provisions enough to get out if he could, and was ordered to move up-river at least one hundred and fifty miles from that camp, and assured that if ever he was seen within that distance of it, any one then present would be justified in shooting him on sight. He left to make his way unaided up the Yukon, to and over the Dyea Pass, more than five hundred miles, in the inclement winter and spring months, and he succeeded so well that he reached Haines Mission when I did, and told the story of the Indian rising which caused so much apprehensive anxiety for many miles of my journey down-river. I heard the story from some of the miners and had the satisfaction, as well, of meeting two of the men who were poisoned. They told me the story as I have related it. They then thought that

Discoverer only did what probably they, under all the circumstances, would have done themselves. It was thought he richly deserved punishment, but as they had no prison in which to confine him, nor any way to detain him for any length of time, all they could do was hang him or banish him. His death they did not wish to be directly responsible for, though many of them felt they were condemning him to death in agreeing to the sentence imposed.

Later on, when dealing with the miners' methods of dispensing justice, we will see how another man for a much smaller offence received a precisely similar sentence.

CHAPTER IV

REMARKS ON MR. OGILVIE'S SURVEY

A FEW remarks on my survey from Pyramid Island in the head of Chilcat Inlet will not be out of place. As there was no certainty that I would be able to reach the International Boundary Line on the Yukon, it was necessary that as far as I went I should approximately, at least, be able to locate my positions. To do this I must begin my survey at a point whose latitude and longitude were pretty well established by reliable authority. In 1867 the now venerable Prof. George Davidson, then in the service of the United States Coast and Geodetic Survey, made a reconnaissance survey of the coast-line wherever practicable along the Alaska front. In 1869 the same gentleman observed the total solar eclipse of that year, August 7th, at a place up the Chilcat River, and while there determined the latitude and longitude of a point in that vicinity. I assumed the position of the island referred to as fixed by him and began my survey there, carrying it over the peninsula to Chilcoot Inlet at Haines Mission, from there across Chilcoot Inlet to the mouth of Dyea Inlet, up it and through the pass at its head to the summit, locating as I went the notable peaks around, and inferring their heights above sea-level from their angles of elevation, and distances from my stations as determined by the method of triangulation. The summit of this pass I found in this way to be 3500 feet above sea, and Lake Lyndeman being 1350 feet below it, is 2150 feet above sea-level. As my measurements were not of a very precise order these heights may not quite agree with the absolute determinations made very recently. My determinations, however, will not prove very far from the absolute truth. My altitude for White Horse was about 2054 feet, and the White Pass Engineering Survey makes it 2084.

The survey was carried from the summit down to where we built our boat, and when that was finished, loaded, and sent on, the work was resumed, and carried without interruption to the International Boundary Line. We resumed work at Lake Bennet July 11th, and reached the boundary line September 14th. The distance is 640 miles. The method of survey was as follows: Two canoes were employed, one of which went ahead picking out good sites for stations. At each station they would land, set up a base rod they carried with them, and wait till the direction or bearing of it in degrees, minutes, and seconds of arc from the preceding station was read by me or my assistant. Also till the small angle subtended by two discs attached to it, which were exactly twenty links of Gunter's chain, or thirteen feet and one-fifth, a part was measured as exactly as possible by a small heliometer micrometer. Then the base men were signalled to go on and select another station, and so on to the end. From the angle subtending the twenty-link base the distance was inferred by the principles of trigonometry. Gunter's links were used because this standard simplified very much the reduction of the distances to chains, and from that to miles. It is hardly necessary to say that with such a short base the distances found were not accurate, but with a good heliometer, such as was used, and carefully repeating the angular measurements, results were obtained that for distances not exceeding a mile at a sight came within a few feet of the accurately measured length. In practice the system was found seldom to exceed an error of one part in a hundred. In this case it was found that the total error between Pyramid Island and the crossing of the Yukon by the boundary line was only three miles in a distance of nearly seven hundred. The system, while not accurate enough to think of determining the position of the boundary line by, was accurate enough to put in the topography along the river and give its length from point to point. The vicinity of the boundary reached, we set about getting up our observatories and winter quarters. This done the men settled down to trying to pass the dreary winter nights as cheerfully as they could, and taking as much exercise as the weather would permit. I settled to my winter's task of getting all the astronomical observations I could to determine as closely as possible the position of the 141st Meridian west of Greenwich. The most accurate determinations of longitude by astronomical methods require the existence of a telegraph line between two points, of one of which the position is required, and that of the other well known. By this method differences of longitude to within ten or twelve feet can easily be determined. The procedure is: At each station an astronomical transit is set up with which to observe with the utmost precision the transits of stars over the meridian of the place, at one, or it may be both, of the stations a standard time-keeper, clock or chronometer, is set up, and nursed so as to give the best possible performance. A list of stars is selected, the transit of which over the meridian of both places is observed, the time of each transit recorded with the utmost accuracy by a chronograph. From the interval of time elapsed between the transits of the stars at the two places the difference of longitude is inferred, for difference of time is difference of longitude, and vice versa. Next to actual measurement of the distance between the two points this is the most accurate method of determining the difference of longitude. As there was no telegraph line to any point on or near the Yukon, and no practicable way of measuring accurately enough from any convenient point to the vicinity of the boundary, the only way open to me was observations on the moon. It affords two methods of determining longitudes, one by getting the exact local time when the moon occults a star, or in other words eclipses it, the other to get the exact local time when the moon transits the meridian of the place. In the first case, if the time of disappearance of the star can be determined within a small fraction of a second, the moon's place can be determined closely enough to give by comparing this place at the exact local time with the place of the moon at their base observatory, as shown in the standard ephemeris of the moon, published annually by the naval service of all the leading countries. As the moon encircles the earth about every twenty-nine days, it, of course, is continually changing its place among the stars, and, at any time if we measure accurately its position with reference to the well-placed stars around it, we know from their place the place of the moon, and by comparing that place with the place given for it in the ephemeris of the nearest standard observatory, in my case Washington, at certain stated hours, we have a measure of the motion of the moon since that time at Washington, and as the moon completes about one twenty-ninth of a circuit in a day, we infer from the noted change of place the difference of time between the place of observation and the standard observatory, wherever it may be. These methods are only about one twenty-ninth as accurate as the method of telegraph and star transit above referred to, and when we consider the natural difficulties of very fine work in the extremely low temperatures in the winter months of those high latitudes, the disproportion is much more, probably sixty to one. When I say that some of my observations were taken when the temperature was lower than fifty below zero, and often when it was lower than forty, and seldom higher than thirty below, one can appreciate the difficulty of getting the most accurate work from even such limited appliances as the transportation facilities at that time afforded. Not only did the temperature add to the personal discomfort, and interfere with bodily freedom through excessive clothing, for one must be very warmly clothed indeed to remain standing still in an open-roofed observatory for two hours in such temperatures, but it also seriously interfered with the instruments used and impaired their delicacy. More especially was this the case with the chronometer. Chronometers are adjusted for temperatures within limits, but the temperatures here were much outside the limits generally accepted by makers.

The one I had was a remarkably good one, but the temperatures it was subjected to in this work was a strain for which it was never intended. If I had had the good fortune to take two with me, one to be kept in the house in as uniform a temperature as possible, the other to be used in taking the observations with, and compared very accurately with the house one before and after observing, I could have reduced the high probable error of my observations very much.

It was arranged before I left Ottawa with Mr. W. F. King, now Chief Astronomer for Canada, that we would observe a series of star occultations, he at Kamloops, British Columbia, and I in the vicinity of the International Boundary Line on the Yukon River, or as near as I could get to it. These occultations extended over the lunations of September–October and October–November, and as the number was large, it was hoped that we would secure enough in common to give a pretty close, for the method, approximation to the exact place. But unfortunately the weather was so cloudy and stormy through those two lunations that I could only observe one of the lot, and that one under such unfavourable circumstances that it was of little value. I had to resort to the method of moon culminations, or moon transits over the meridian of the place referred to. I was fortunate enough to get twenty-two of these in the November–December, December–January, and January–

February lunations. That number, if taken in an up-to-date observatory, equipped with the most refined instruments, would be expected to give an average result within a few hundred feet of the truth, but with a small portable astronomical transit, of which I had only the telescope, mounted on a stump instead of the usual stand, I could not look for a very exact result. The stand weighed four hundred pounds, a serious item of transport where everything had to be carried for miles over the pass on men's backs, serious enough to set me planning to dispense with it, which I did by devising a set of brasses to be fastened on a stump of suitable size, and on these the telescope could be mounted in the same way as on the stand. These reduced the weight from over four hundred to less than eighty pounds. Trusting to the reports I read of the size of the trees along the river I did not expect any trouble in finding my tree, a diameter of only twenty-two inches being required. When the time to mount the instrument came a three days' hunt in the vicinity of the boundary line found only one tree approaching the necessary diameter at the requisite height, about five feet, and that one being only eighteen inches I had to reinforce it with blocks on the sides to get the proper support for my brasses. The position of this tree determined the site of our winter quarters, for we had to be near the observatory. It stood on the side of a steep hill, which occasioned both inconvenience and inaccuracy, for it was found that the stump swayed up or down the hill with a change of temperature, and seldom was absolutely stationary. Result, the transit had to be levelled every evening just before beginning work, but it continued to swing during work. At the close of the observations and their reduction, the resultant position was marked by cutting the line through the woods north and south of the river for a distance. Then a survey was made up the Fortymile river and the boundary line marked on it.

In 1889 the United States determined to test the position I had given the boundary line on the Yukon and Fortymile, also to locate it on the Porcupine, so two parties were sent in, one under Mr. McGrath to observe on the Yukon and Fortymile, and the other under Mr. Turner to observe on the Porcupine. I was requested by the Minister of the Interior of Canada to prepare a report of my operations for the information of those men, and to furnish such advice as I thought would be useful to them, which I did. Both parties made their way by the Alaska Commercial Company's boat from San Francisco to St. Michael, and from there on the same company's new river steamer *Arctic* to the seat of their operations. Both those gentlemen had to use the same methods of getting the longitude as I did, and Mr. McGrath made use of my winter quarters and observatory on the Yukon. He remained two winters in the country, getting some thirteen observations in that time, the result of which was that the line as I had marked it was accepted until such time as better methods of observing could be utilized in the vicinity. This was done four years ago by the star transit and electric telegraph method, by both American and Canadian parties, and the old line that stood as the boundary for nearly twenty years, and that is a long time as the world moves now, was found to be only a few score yards from where it ought to be.

Its exact intersection with the Yukon River was found, and from that point a Joint Commission of American and Canadian surveyors is carrying it south to the Pacific Ocean, marking it by permanent monuments on the hill-tops, and cutting a wide swath through the woods between. When the line to the Pacific is finished in this way it will then be carried north to the Arctic in the same way.

The distance from ocean to ocean on this line is about seven hundred miles, and the Yukon crossing is very nearly the middle point in the distance. When finished it will be a well-defined white ribbon during the winter, and as the growth of trees and shrubs is remarkably slow in the latitudes it traverses, it will be many years, it might be said generations, before it will require reopening. At the present rate of advance with the work it will likely be seven or eight years more before it is completed.

I have previously stated that the determination of the boundary line on the Porcupine found the Hudson's Bay Company post, which had been moved up that river from the mouth, still in American territory, and it was abandoned.

CHAPTER V

TRADING AND TRADING POSTS ON THE RIVER

BEFORE reviewing the trading posts, and posts generally on the river after the transfer of the territory to the United States by Russia, we will glance at the attempt of the Western Union Telegraph Company to establish a line to, and across, Bering Straits, and from there to the west of Europe. This company's exploring parties were in the Yukon valley 1866–7 looking for a route for the globe-circling wire, as it was intended to be. The failure of the Atlantic cable of 1858 was responsible for this attempt, and the successful laying by the Great Eastern of the cable in 1866 rendered it useless; but it was a year after before the news reached the explorers. Of those explorers one, Dall, left his name on the page of history, through his writings. Another, Michael Labarge, of Montreal, Canada, will be remembered by the beautiful lake called after him on the upper Yukon, though he never saw it, but hearing of it, he described it to some parties who, afterwards reaching it, called it after him.

He remained in the country trading for some time after this.

In 1868, closely following the transfer from Russia, the San Francisco firm of Hutchinson, Kohl & Co. bought out the Russian-American Company trading in Alaska, in its entirety, and took possession of all its posts and effects. The firm, however, soon changed its name, and became incorporated as the Alaska Commercial Company. It retained this name till 1901, when it merged with a company of very recent origin, the Alaska Exploration Company, and the name of the joint concern became the Northern Commercial Company. It is to-day probably the strongest trading company in all the North-West. The Alaska Commercial Company established posts along the river as suited the convenience of trade, and for a time occupied the Hudson's Bay abandoned post at the mouth of the Porcupine in charge of Moses Mercier, of Montreal, whose brother Francois was in general charge at St. Michael. The Hudson's Bay style of dealing with the Indians, however, had encouraged them in habits the new people thought slow, too slow for modern business methods. The Indian did not then, nor does he yet, care to do business in the rush method; he likes to come to the post, and first have a solemn shake hands all round, then after a short talk he likes to take a friendly smoke (the trader furnishing the tobacco), then as much to eat as he can get, and the more tea to drink with it the better; after a day or two, or as much of this as your patience will stand, he is ready to trade, but you must be very diplomatic in concealing your feelings of annoyance, or you may ruin business. The agent at Fort Yukon could not get accustomed to the Indian style, for it was that and nothing more which the Hudson's Bay people had fallen into, and so thinking it easier to break in a new crowd, moved his post about one hundred and ninety miles up the Yukon, where he established himself; and being French-Canadian called the post Belle Isle, or Beautiful Island. The United States military post Fort Egbert (Eagle) is on the site of this historic trading post. In 1871 Napoleon Leroy—better known as Jack—McQuesten established for the company Fort Reliance, about six miles below where Dawson now is. He came into the territory in 1873, and entered the service of the company the following summer. In the fall of that year Arthur Harper joined McQuesten in the trading business, and in 1875 Harper and Alfred H. Mayo, who was also trading with them, were in charge of Fort Reliance. They had some trouble with the Indians, who were not as amenable to reason then as since the white brother has become so numerous, and they had to leave. Before going they concealed ("cached" the local term is), as well as they could, all the supplies in the place, among other things a mixture of arsenic and grease, which they used as rat poison. After they left the Indians looted the post, and finding this compound proceeded to mix it with some flour and make bread. The result was, two old women and one blind girl died. In the fall McQuesten came up with an outfit for the store, and of course had to make terms with the Indians. After a pow-wow it was agreed that the Indians would pay for what they took out of the store if McQuesten would pay for the women poisoned—a very one-sided settlement we would think when we consider the Suffragette movement of the present day.

After McQuesten had billed them to the limit for the goods appropriated, he asked, almost in terror, we may suppose, how much they thought the women worth. A short calculation at current rates fixed the prices as follows : the two old women were not valued at all, being a nuisance, and for the young one, ten skins, the current terms of the country, *about six dollars*, was demanded. This amount was cheerfully paid, and some presents given besides, and the prompt payment and kindliness established the very best of feeling.

In 1886 Harper, McQuesten, and Mayo established a post at the mouth of the Stewart to accommodate the miners who were gathering on that stream, and following the discovery of coarse gold on the Fortymile River, they erected at the

BEGINNING OF CIRCLE CITY, ALASKA, 1894

mouth of that river in September, 1887, another post.

In 1889 Harper left the firm. It had been trading on commission for the Alaska Commercial Company, and the parties continued with this company on the same terms, but independently of each other.

In 1893 McQuesten outfitted some men and sent them down to prospect on Birch Creek in American territory. The venture was successful, and the following spring McQuesten took all the supplies that could be spared from the camp at Fortymile, and at the point on the Yukon most convenient to the new mining ground founded Circle City, because it was in the vicinity of the Arctic Circle. It is hardly near enough it, however, to deserve the distinction, being about eighty-eight miles up the Yukon from the Circle, and nearly a degree in latitude south of it.

While McQuesten was founding Circle City, Harper opened business at Selkirk on the site of Robert Campbell's old post; he also built a new post opposite to the mouth of Sixtymile Creek, which he named Ogilvie, after the writer. This was done in pursuance of a resolution made by him and McQuesten after my first visit to the country, to name any future posts they might establish in Canadian territory after Canadian officials, notably those who had visited the country, and as I was the first they met, they began with myself. Dawson followed, being called after Dr. Dawson, late Director of the Canadian Geological Survey.

In 1892 Capt. J. J. Healy, to whom we have referred, organized in Chicago a company to trade on the Yukon, and in Alaska generally, which was named the "North American Transportation and Trading Company." In the summer of that year he had built for the company its first river steamer, the *Porteous B. Weare*, after its first President. It was intended that this steamer with an outfit of supplies would reach Fortymile that fall, but ice was encountered at Nulato, and the boat and party had to winter there, reaching Fortymile in 1893. Just below the mouth of that river, Healy proceeded to erect large storehouses and trading shops, also living quarters. This post Healy named Cudahy, after a prominent member of the company. In 1895 both this company and the Alaska Commercial Company put up the buildings at Circle City necessary for their business. As soon as Dawson was founded both companies erected very large storehouses and shops there. As those big companies have to store in a month, or two at most, all they require for a year, their storehouses have to be much larger than the same amount of business would require where year-round transport facilities exist.

FORTYMILE 1895

STEAMBOAT DEVELOPMENT ON THE RIVER

We will refer in brief to the history of steamboat navigation on this river. The first steamer to furrow its waters was fittingly named *Yukon*. In 1869 John Parrott and other merchants of San Francisco sent a brig to St. Michael with a trading outfit, and the material to make a small river steamer. The boat was built that season and made a trip up to and past Fort Yukon. One of her passengers was Capt. C. W. Raymond, already mentioned. Soon after the Alaska Commercial Company bought out this firm, and the boat became the property of that company. The steamer *St. Michael* was the second boat on the river, and in 1871 she went up as far, it is said, as Selkirk, trading as she went, and returned with a valuable cargo of furs. In the fall of 1882, Ed. Schieffelin, the discoverer of the "Tombstone Mine" in Arizona, arrived at St. Michael with a party of five men, of whom one was Professor Jacobson of the Royal Berlin Museum, another was Henry de Wolfe who kindly furnished me with a lot of information about the early days on the lower river through an article he wrote for the *San Francisco Bulletin* of September 18th, 1887, a copy of which he sent me, and from which I quote in this record. I may add that Mr. de Wolfe got many of his facts from the people of the Alaska Commercial Company, at its head office in San Francisco. I also have in my possession quite a lengthy article written specially for me by *Jack* McQuesten, as the old timers loved to call him, in which he gives me his recollections of the beginning of things on the river, of which he is sometimes called the "Father," so intimately associated was he with the mining development there. In both articles the Schieffelin party is referred to with some difference of detail, but not enough to call in question the main facts. As this is not intended to be more than a concise statement of the most prominent features, it would be a waste of time to attempt an analysis of the records; it is sufficient for our purpose now to say that Schieffelin brought with him the lumber and machinery for a small stern-wheel steamer which he called the *New Racket*, and with which he and party in 1883 ascended the river, neither record says how far. The party, with the exception of one, went out in the fall. The boat was sold to Harper, McQuesten & Co., in other words the Alaska Commercial Company, and for several years did them good service.

In the fall of 1887, when my party was busy putting up our winter quarters, to be precise, September 22nd, we heard just around a bend two miles below us the exhaust puff of a stern-wheel steamer. We had learned at Fortymile that the *New Racket* would, barring accident, be up before long, so concluded it was she, but somehow she did not seem to materialize, and we began to wonder if the river was haunted, for we could see no sign of her smoke over the woods, and we expected to see clouds of smoke and steam, judging from the rapidity and force of her exhaust, which, strange to say, continued for only a minute or two at a time, with much longer intervals between. We had first noticed the noise early in the morning, and about nine were on the point of starting down to learn what the mystery was, when her nose appeared over the point of the bend, and though it was less than two miles away she took more than two hours to reach our camp, where the captain (Al. Mayo) tied up for awhile, and told us of his difficulty—leaking tubes, plenty of them, and leaking badly too. The result of which was they could not keep up steam, and the programme was reduced to going ashore for a few minutes, bottling up steam as high as the danger mark, slipping out, and letting her go till steam was exhausted, then to the bank again for more steam, and so on all day. They had no expander to close the leaks, nor any other appliance that would help, and though only some thirty-seven miles from Fortymile it looked like a ten to twelve days' voyage. Of course we were consulted about the difficulty, and as I had once or twice before seen others in the same predicament, I suggested a remedy I had seen tried with a measure of success, namely, to get dry wood, make tight-fitting plugs, and drive them into the worst leaking tubes. The escaping water soon expanded the wood to such an extent that the leak closed. The heating surface of the tube was lost, but it did not leak, and if the leak had been greater than the steam-making power of the tube there was a gain. This was tried with the worst tubes, with such success that after dinner with us the boat went merrily on her way, not stopping as far as we could hear her, though the steam necessarily went down through loss of heating surface. Arrived at Fortymile she found a number of miners anxiously waiting her to essay a trip to Stewart River, and up it as far as the season would permit. When coarse gold was discovered on the Fortymile River in 1886 the rush was to it, but the prospecting done in 1887 showed that though the gold was coarse it was not so uniformly spread over the surface as on Stewart River, and very much more difficult to get, so a number who had not struck it rich on the Fortymile were compelled to look for a grubstake, and knowing they could make the stake, if they reached it in time, determined to spend the fall and winter on the Stewart. Arrangements had been made with the owners before the boat's arrival to have the trial of reaching the river made, taking as many prospectors and their outfits as could find room on board. It is hardly necessary to say the number was not large, eighteen or

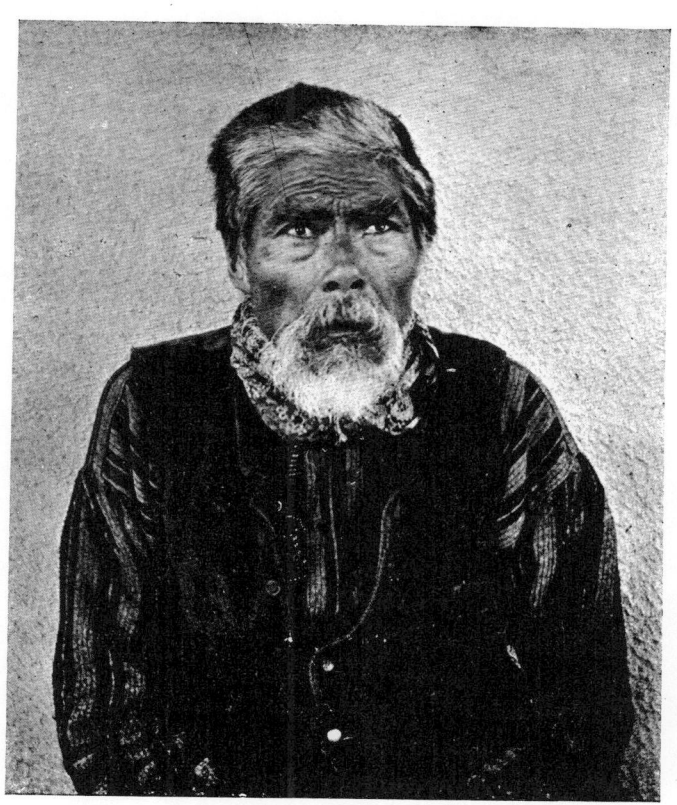

CHIEF CHARLEY

twenty, yet the small steamer was so crowded that they had to sleep in relays. Among them was a well-known *character* nicknamed " Long John," few knowing him by any other title. "Long John" was an Irish Canadian whom I had met at home many years before and well remembered his innate Irish humour, which he delivered in a rich Irish brogue of a not too " broguey " style, that made most things he said inexpressibly comical. He was famed all over the Territory for his fun-making qualities, which being absolutely unstudied were all the more amusing. You could depend on John for a laugh any time, under any conditions, and the yarns I have heard of him and the things I have heard him say would make an entertaining book in themselves. Now, the boat's leaking boiler tubes had been fixed as well as possible at Fortymile, and she sailed under Capt. Mayo, whom the boys admired for his fondness for a joke, especially practical ones. For a day or so the boat made good time, loaded as she was, and against the current, and high hopes of reaching the Stewart and taking out the needed grubstake were entertained. The distance to the Stewart from Fortymile is about one hundred and thirty miles, and half the course had been covered when the trouble with the tubes began again, and the high hopes leaked away with the leaking tubes. Try as they would, they made but little progress; still the miners urged Mayo to get them to the mouth of the Stewart if possible. He was as willing to go as they were to ask, and continued until it became evident to the most sanguine that the task was impossible. While "Long John" and his relay were slumbering, Capt. Mayo called a council of all awake, and frankly told them that they were making such poor progress that even if they continued it would be so late when the mouth of the Stewart was reached that he had little hopes they would accomplish anything, and to attempt going up the latter river with the steamer as she was would be folly. It was unanimously agreed that the steamer be turned and the best speed possible be made back to Fortymile. When the time for a change of sleepers came all except "Long John" were quietly awakened, beckoned to come out, and the change in direction explained to them, then John was called. As soon as he came outside he noticed that the boat was making great speed, and he remarked on it in language as picturesque as the scenery around, and highly amusing to his auditors. There was no hurry to get to sleep, all were admiring with John the new-found speed, and explaining to him in original detail just how the trick was accomplished, and laughing volcanically at his animadversions on the executive of the boat for not having found the way sooner to ensure their arrival at their destination. After easing his mind he got out his pipe and proceeded to take a smoke on it, occasionally removing the pipe to remark that they were "goin' like h—l" now, or some kindred ejaculation, and then bestowing a left-handed blessing on the captain and the crew for not "thryin' that way before," this would be followed by some grave calculations as to "whin" they would reach the Stewart, and how far they would get up. All this provoked more laughter than those who do not know John and his kind would think possible. After quite a long smoke John looked at the trees flying swiftly past, then at the water, then would look indescribably serious for awhile, which would be followed by another keen look at the trees and water. At last he had mastered the problem, and taking his pipe out of his mouth, jumping to his feet and flinging his arms aloft, he shouted in a tone that rang throughout the boat, "Julius Cæsar's ghost, boys! it's down we'r goin'! What the h—l has happened?" and so on in the most lurid language imaginable, while every soul on board was in convulsions of laughter. After the joke was explained to John, he enjoyed it as much as any one, and concurred heartily in the judgment that turned the boat.

It is hardly necessary to say that those three boats, *Yukon*, *St. Michael*, and *New Racket*, were not large. They could not be, under the conditions. Seventy to eighty feet in length, and fourteen to twenty wide, with a depth of hull from three to four feet was about the average.

As a rule, however, they were fitted with powerful machinery for their size. With the crew, a fair supply of wood, and a few passengers they were crowded. As a transport motor they shoved small barges, each capable of carrying about ten tons. With four or five of these in tow the *Yukon* could make a round trip from St. Michael to any point in the vicinity of the boundary line in about a month, the up-stream time being twenty days. When these boats first plied on the river they were a great surprise and curiosity to the natives. When the surprise ceased the curiosity became an annoyance to the people on board, for the Indian is only a child in such matters, and the less he understands anything the more curious he is about it, and getting in a man's way to see what he is doing is as natural to him as to live. Whenever a boat would call at a new camp, there was always a crowd to get on board as soon as she touched shore, and swarm all over her regardless of the convenience or comfort of any one. Capt. Mayo told me of what a nuisance this often was to him, and how difficult it was to get the natives to do anything till after they had glutted their eyes looking at things, and if he or one of the crew touched anything, or adjusted any part of the machinery, that thing or part must be looked at all over before they would leave it, unless pushed away, and if he pushed one out of the way another immediately stepped into the place if he

INDIAN CAMP AT FORT SELKIRK, 1887

could, giving the evicted one a grin of contempt as he did so. Mayo was fond of playing practical jokes, and he retained a keen enjoyment of them for years after. I remember his once telling me, and laughing as heartily about it as if it had just happened, of a trick he played on a lot of natives to get them out of his way on the *New Racket* the first year he was running her. Coming up on the lower river he was hailed one day by a large encampment of Indians who wanted to get some supplies, they alleged, but most of all they wanted to see the white man's big boat. Between the water edge and the bank was a broad strip of quicksand, over which lay a stratum of half-dried mud, upon which sticks had been laid to support water-carriers on their way to the river. Mayo ran the boat's nose into this, and as soon as the gang-plank was laid on the quagmire the Indians, man and boy, literally swarmed on board in such numbers that there was danger of keeling the steamer so much that she would take water and sink. Say what he could, do what he might, Mayo could not make the Indians understand that there was any danger. They had come aboard to see, and see they would! They were determined once and for all time to learn the secret of the mighty power which pushed so many boats against the strong waters where they had so much trouble to take one small one. Mayo saw that something must be done, and done at once, or a catastrophe might, probably would, overwhelm them. Pushing his way to the boiler room, followed by as many natives as could make headway, he groped for the safety valve beam, the old lever and weight kind, which he raised as high as he could. The result exceeded his expectations. It was magical. The blast of the pent-up steam through the safety scape-pipe seemed literally to sweep over the entire vessel, blowing every native from where he was, in the direction he was facing, into the water, or wherever else he could get away from the monster on which he stood. The entire encampment on shore, children, women, and old men, fled for their very lives, and those in the river and on the quagmire followed as fast as they could, terror-driven at a speed nothing else could provoke. Mayo said he never laughed so in his life before, and thought he never would again, which must have been "laughing some." He told me one old man was standing on the upper deck when the valve let go. He was facing the shore, and sprang with such force from the deck that he landed on the quagmire, the crust of which he went through, and sank almost to his armpits. In the first uproar and rush they did not hear him, but when the crowd vanished, and they could hear him, his calls for help and yells of terror seemed to come from the most profound depths of his soul. As soon as the first paroxysm of laughter was over, Mayo and the crew fished the old man out, who at once put as much distance between himself and the roaring monster as he possibly could, and Mayo told me he did it in a style and at a rate that would have won a Marathon. The boat was untied and proceeded on her way, we may suppose much to the satisfaction of the natives. I have several times been told of this trick being resorted to, to clear a mill, or other factory on the frontiers, of unwelcome natives, with a result just as gratifying and amusing to the operator as in this case.

In 1888 it was evident that the business on the river required more capacious steamers to keep pace with it, and accordingly the Alaska Commercial Company had the steamer *Arctic* built at St. Michael's in 1889. She was finished in time to make her maiden trip that season, and took as two of her passengers Mr. McGrath and Mr. Turner, who were, as we have mentioned, going to observe for the position of the International Boundary Line on the Yukon and Porcupine rivers. The *Arctic* was not a large steamer as such craft go now, yet she was a great advance on the *Yukon*. Her length was about one hundred and forty feet, by about twenty-eight feet beam, and six feet depth. She made good time on the river, and, as far as I know to the contrary, still holds the record for voyages during one season on the Yukon River. In 1895, piloted by Capt. Wm. Moore, of Victoria, B.C., she made one run from Anvik, about four hundred miles from St. Michael, to Fortymile, and four runs from St. Michael to Fortymile and return. This has never, as far as I have learned, been repeated. It means more than fourteen thousand miles in a little more than two months, over a course then but little known, where the pilot's memory was his only chart, and that chart included more than fifteen hundred miles of tortuous channel—a channel varying with each shower of rain, and but few showers affecting more than a fraction of its length at one time. The next steamer on the run was the North American Transportation and Trading Company's steamer already mentioned, the *Porteous B. Weare*, put on in 1892. This boat was slightly larger than the *Arctic*, but not quite so fast. In 1895 the Alaska Commercial Company put on the *Alice*, and a sister boat, the *Bella*, not quite so large, was built and launched, but did not make the run that year. The *Alice* was a respectable boat as they go to-day, her length being one hundred and sixty-five feet, beam thirty-two feet, and depth eight feet. These latter boats were intended to push large barges carrying as much freight as the steamer, and were fitted with powerful engines for their size. The North American Company about the same time put on a sister ship to the *Weare*, the *John J. Healy*. All those boats ran on the lower river, the *Arctic* going only once as high as Selkirk, the *Alice* to

Ogilvie, and the *Bella* to the mouth of White River.

Following the discovery of the Klondike, and the founding of Dawson, many other steamers and some much larger were put on. Several small boats were put on from Dawson up, some of which plied between the head of Lake Bennet and the head of the Canon and White Horse Rapids, past which there were two lines of tramway of the most primitive construction, made of the material found to hand, ties laid at intervals of from three or four to eight or ten feet, as they were convenient ; rails of wood were hewed from the poles found beside the roadway and spiked at long intervals to the ties. Occasionally the outside rail was faced with iron plates in very sharp curves. The tramcars were mounted on cast-iron wheels of the simplest construction, and harmonized in primeval simplicity with the roadway. The systems, or any part of them, could hardly be called " a thing of beauty," and were not destined "to be a joy for ever," yet there was a quiet charm about the lines as they wound through ravines, around gravel ridges, to the sides of which they clung but feebly, and braved the terrors of the rapids below at many points by jutting over the bank. The charm of distant and more sublime scenery was not wanting, for at the most unexpected places wondrously pleasing vistas of distant snow-clad peaks would rise out of the woods and shrubbery as if by magic. The run of four miles over these lines on cars that might have been made in the Stone Age, three or four of which were drawn by a horse, was a glimpse of the legendary, and it is almost a pity that modern rush brushed them aside. Most of both lines exist to-day almost as they were built, and if ever necessity drove us to use them a few hours' time would put them in working order.

The Canadian Development Company put on the run from Dawson to the foot of the White Horse Rapids three steamers of good size and power, the *Canadian, Columbian*, and *Victorian*. They were rather heavily built, and too bluff in the model for the run, but they did wonderfully good service nevertheless, and running them taught every pilot on the upper river how to navigate it.

The White Pass Company, which practically controls the traffic above Dawson, has four very comfortable steamers, good freighters, and comfortable passenger boats. They are swift and graceful. The dimensions are about one hundred and sixty feet long, thirty-two feet beam, and six feet deep. This company has freight boats besides.

Before leaving this subject it may be of interest to give the dimensions of the largest boats on the run from Dawson down. We cite the three largest of the Northern Commercial Company's

ALASKA COMMERCIAL CO.'S STEAMER "SUSIE"

boats, the *Hannah*, *Sarah*, and *Susie*. Length two hundred and twenty-two feet eight inches, beam forty-two feet, depth six feet two inches, net register tonnage six hundred and thirty-nine, indicated horse-power one thousand, which drives them about seventeen miles an hour in still water.

The North American Company has several boats almost as large, and as comfortable for passengers.

There are several small boats owned by private individuals on both the upper and lower runs, but as steamers they are not worth specializing.

CHAPTER VI

GOLD DISCOVERIES AND MINING

WE now come to the feature that has made this region famed, and but for which it might have lain dormant till the crush of humanity had pushed the race into the outlying parts of the earth: Gold! GOLD!! Robert Campbell knew sixty years ago that there was gold in the gravel at his trading-post on the Pelly and Yukon; but he was not a miner, and indeed there were few in the world who could then have extracted successfully the gold from the gravel. The "rocker" and "sluice box" were not so familiar as now, and the gold would have been plentiful indeed that would have diverted those grim pioneers from the chase for furs, to which they devoted life and limb. Nearly two generations ago a missionary took up his abode in that far-away region. He died recently at Fort McPherson near the mouth of Mackenzie River. In the middle years of the past century he lived and laboured among the Indians on the Porcupine and the Yukon in that vicinity. His work called him as far up the Yukon as the river afterwards called the Fortymile, and from it over to the head of the Tanana. In his journeyings he crossed the sources of the since famous Birch Creek, the Circle City field, and on one of its branches he found gold. As he had his headquarters at Fort Yukon the knowledge was common there, but fur traders do not understand gold mining. The methods are to them a sealed book, and as the trading seasons are strenuous, though short, they had not much time to devote to mining even if they would. Even the early miners on the Yukon, men whose life business it was, and learned in all the lore of the craft, did not think it possible to mine in the winter, until forced to that conclusion by long experience in the country. In the year 1859 a young man of the city of Toronto, Canada, entered the service of the Hudson's Bay Company and was sent to the other end of the world, as it was considered then, to the Company's most distant post, Fort Yukon. In the fall of the year soon after his arrival he wrote a long letter home giving a minute account of his journey of nearly five thousand miles. On October 2nd, 1864, he wrote again, and told of the fur trade and its dog expeditions in the winter, and boat voyages in the summer after furs. He dwelt with feeling on the fear of meeting some of the Russian parties on the river below the fort where he often went, and though he was not afraid of an encounter he was anxious about it.

The idea appeared to be that there would be a collision, and the strongest party would take all the furs.

I have copies of both these letters, and though all the contents are interesting the following paragraph is extremely so as foreshadowing the future of the Yukon : " I had some thoughts of digging the gold here, but am not sure about it. I do not think it is in paying quantities at the fort, but if I could only get time to make an expedition up the Yukon, I expect we should find it in abundance, but I am always on the voyage or busy at the fort during the summer, *and in the winter nothing can be done in the way of gold-hunting.* I think that next fall, after arriving from my trip down the Yukon, I shall be able to go up the river. There is a small river not far from here that the minister, the Rev. McDonald, saw so much gold on a year or two ago that he could have gathered it with a spoon. I have often wished to go, but can never find the time. Should I find gold in paying quantities I may turn gold-digger, but this is merely a *last resort when I can do no better.*" A last resort! how it sounds now, and it was not sarcasm, nor moralizing on the vanity of riches either. A last resort to a young man on a yearly stipend of not more than two hundred dollars and such board and lodging as the country afforded. To the miners of the Yukon it, well! they have a last resort

GOLD DISCOVERIES AND MINING

by which they may relieve themselves about it, but it is doubtful if they can express themselves completely. A last resort where you could gather gold with a spoon! The small river referred to is quite evidently Birch Creek, and the time of the discovery by the missionary must have been in 1862 or '63, or fourteen or fifteen years after Campbell knew that there was gold at Selkirk, but it could not be gathered with a spoon.

ARTHUR HARPER, THE PIONEER MINER

The first man who thought of trying the Yukon as a mining field, so far as we know, was Arthur Harper. Born in the county of Antrim, Ireland, in 1835, he left it while yet a boy to try his luck in America. He spent some time on the Atlantic seaboard of the United States, but being of an adventurous nature he drifted westward to the Pacific slope goldfields, and in the latter years of the sixth decade of the past century was in British Columbia. Fortune did not favour him overmuch, and he looked about him for new fields, untried, to renew his quest. He had possessed himself of a copy of Arrowsmith's—London—map of British North America, which gave a pretty thorough representation of the topography of the country covered by the Hudson's Bay Company, from whom Arrowsmith got much of his information. A study of this map led Harper to believe that there was a much more extensive gold-bearing field in the north than any one suspected. He saw the head-waters of the two most important branches of the Mackenzie, the Liard and Peace, flowing from well-defined auriferous areas in British Columbia; he saw the Yukon, through its affluents, rising in the same field, and he convinced himself that if gold were plentiful on the sources of the Mackenzie, it was just as plentiful on the Yukon. Not only did he convince himself, but he convinced four others sufficiently to test the theory with him—Frederick Hart, a fellow-countryman from the same county, and of about the same age; George Finch, a Canadian from the city of Kingston; Andrew Kansellar, a German, and Samuel Wilkinson, an Englishman. These men, in September, 1872, equipped themselves for a long journey and a protracted stay in the wilderness to the north of them, and started from Manson Creek, on the head-waters of the Peace, for the, to them, unknown. There was no literature then they could conveniently get to enlighten them. The Hudson's Bay Company records and publications, such as they were, were not much known outside of the service, and besides dealt almost exclusively with the fur trade. In a large boat of their own building they went down the Peace and over the Mountain Portage, twelve difficult, soul-trying miles, and continued on the now placid Peace

ARTHUR HARPER, PIONEER MINER

from there to Half-way River. On the way they met a party of engineers exploring for the Canadian Pacific Railway Survey, then just begun, and to assist them exchanged boats with them, the engineers having ponderous dug-out cottonwood canoes, which were awkward, unsafe, and difficult to drive. Now why Harper and his party did not go down the Peace instead of the way they went is difficult to understand. By following it down they would have had much less trouble than they had, and reached their destination on the Mackenzie much sooner. At that time mining in the winter was not thought of, and their route could not benefit them in that way. Half-way River is about midway between the Mountain Rapids and Fort St. John, hence its name. Mountain Rapids are constituted by the passage of the Peace through the Rocky Mountains, and to pass them there is a twelve-mile portage, very trying and difficult, and what path there had been cut through the woods was then grown over again with underbrush, and made as impassable as the native woods; indeed, more so in parts. Harper and party supposed that Half-way River came from the watershed common to the Peace and Liard rivers, and so went up it as far as the dug-out canoes would permit, not very far at that late time of the year, and there waited till winter set in, when they rigged sleds and hauled their stuff over to, and down, another stream which they could only guess joined the Liard. They sleighed so far down that they felt sure of safe canoe navigation, and there camped till spring, building a large elevated cache in which to store their provisions, and spending their time getting as much fresh meat as possible. In the spring they made as many dug-out canoes as were necessary to carry the party and provisions down-stream. The canoes were made of cottonwood poplar trees, which grow to a very large size on the Liard River and its tributaries. The word Liard is French for that species of cottonwood, and as there are extensive groves of it along the banks of that stream, and also on its tributaries, the river took its name from the timber, being so called by the French-Canadian voyageurs of the Hudson's Bay Company. I have seen trees of that variety on the bank of the river not less than five feet in diameter at the ground, and quite one hundred and fifty feet high. At one point I saw a specimen so tall, straight, and clear of limbs, though not among the largest I had seen, that I had it cut down to measure it, and found it four feet four inches across the stump, three feet from the ground, and ninety-two feet to the first limb, where it was eighteen inches in diameter, the top part being over forty feet in length. In 1891 I passed over the route followed by Harper and party, but in the contrary direction, and though this was nineteen years afterwards, I found the cache they built and the frames for their tents in a good state of preservation.

The river they fell on is now marked on our maps " Sikanni Chief River," a leading tributary of the Nelson, which is one of the main branches of the Liard.

At the mouth of the Nelson, Harper and party met another party of three who were also thinking of going to the Yukon. The members of this party were Leroy Napoleon McQuesten, previously known as " Jack," Alfred H. Mayo, and James McKnipp. It is well to state here that I had a number of long interviews with Harper about this journey, which I put in writing, read over to him, reviewing and correcting until I got a version that satisfied him. I afterwards read this to Fred Hart, and he, while agreeing with it so far as the salient features were concerned, made a few objections in detail, but only such as would be due to difference of character in looking at things. Substantially, he agreed with Harper. As I have already said, McQuesten also favoured me with a memorandum written by himself, but in his case I had not the opportunity of talking the matter over with him and comparing his statements with others I had heard and read. As might naturally be expected, McQuesten differs from Harper in some respects, and at this point there is a difference. McQuesten says he and his associates had wintered there to go to the Yukon in the spring, and "they (Harper and the others) concluded to come along," which would imply that Harper and friends were his followers, instead of, as Harper stated it to me, being the leaders in the movement. Both Harper and Hart were quite clear on this point; they left the upper Peace in British Columbia to try both the Mackenzie and the Yukon for gold, and their subsequent course bears out this idea; then, too, Harper and Hart gave me their memoranda about fifteen years before McQuesten did. I do not imply any intentional inaccuracy on Mr. McQuesten's part, for I believe he is incapable of wilful misrepresentation, yet it would seem from the nature of the two memoranda that the chances are in favour of Harper and Hart. I must say, in justice to Mr. McQuesten, that I asked him for a record of things in the Yukon at the same time that I interviewed Harper and Hart, and he told me that he had regularly chronicled events of note for many years, but had loaned his records to a would-be author of a history of the region. He had tried often to have his manuscript back, but had not succeeded. He would, however, try again, and if successful lend it to me to copy. He never got it, but years after when I wrote to him asking for a statement, he sent me what he recollected.

McQuesten was born in Maine, whence his parents moved to Illinois when he was a child.

GOLD DISCOVERIES AND MINING

In his boyhood he went north and west, finally landing in the Hudson's Bay country, where he was employed by it for awhile. The work did not suit his tastes, so he took up the fur trade on his own account. Nearly all the supplies for the Athabasca and Peace River regions came in by British Columbia, and in that way McQuesten became acquainted with the traffic routes in that province, and occasionally traded with the mining camps he passed, and when he met Harper at the mouth of the Nelson they recalled earlier meetings.

Whatever may have been McQuesten's plans as to making his way to Yukon, he appears to have changed them here, for he gave Harper his large boat in exchange for the dug-outs. One of the Harper party at this point, Wilkinson, left the rest to make his way up the Liard in search of gold, believing he would find it sooner and easier on the Liard than by going to the Yukon. One of the items of Harper's outfit was a five-gallon keg of strong black rum, and at every Hudson's Bay post visited this was tapped and a drink passed round. His recollections of some of the results were amusing, and he used to repeat them in humorous style. At one place a large Highland Scotchman who was handed the keg to take it to the house did not wait for that, but drawing the bung cork put it to his mouth, and before any one could interfere had taken a veritable *drink*, not a glass. The result was somewhat amusing, if not a little brutal. In a short time he was wildly intoxicated, and turned berserker, defying all creation to come on and have it out with him. Being a giant in strength, there was a well-manifested inclination shown to let him have it all as he wished, and as no one came near him, he seized a large train dog that was looking on, and taking the front legs in one hand and the hind ones in the other he flung the brute around his neck, the dog howling the while as only those wild wolfish dogs can howl. The human brute seemed to find enjoyment in this, for he marched around the fort square, howling in unison with the dog. No one was anxious to interfere, and the performance was kept up till exhaustion and sleep overtook the man, and he slept the sleep of the unrighteous till Harper and his party left. Harper thought this the most unique display he had ever witnessed, and often recalled it with mingled feelings. On the way down the Mackenzie, which passed without incident of note, the party prospected for gold frequently, but found no colours till they reached the Peel. This large stream drains the country between the Mackenzie and Yukon, and there is no doubt that its head-waters come from the gold-bearing area adjacent to the Klondike, and other streams flowing into the Yukon. It joins the Mackenzie in its delta, which is common to both rivers, and in this Harper told me he found fair

GOLD DISCOVERIES AND MINING

prospects. In giving me the results of his prospecting on this journey he always summed it about as follows. On the Peace everywhere colours were found more or less, on the Liard colours, on the Mackenzie nothing, on the Peel fair prospects, on the Porcupine some colours, and on the Yukon prospects everywhere. From Fort McPherson, at the junction of the Peel with the Mackenzie, they made their way over to the Porcupine by going up a small river tributary to the former stream, now marked on our maps "Rat River," about forty-five miles. The first twenty from the mouth is of moderate current, but the next twenty-four or five is a continuous rapid—the fall in the distance being more than twelve hundred feet. In low water in the summer the stream is so shallow in the rapids that the only way to get a boat of even the lightest draught up is to walk beside it, and pull it around rocks and over them. The boat may be hard on a rock while the men around it are in three or four feet of water. In 1888 I went down it in very light draught canoes in the spring freshet and still found it difficult enough to get along safely. A portage of eight miles leads from this stream to Bells River, which is a branch of the Porcupine, and once on this, all trouble is over, there being nothing worse than a quickening of the current here and there. Following this route, which, by the way, was known as the Edmonton Route during the Klondike rush, because Edmonton was the jumping-off place on it, that is the last touch with modern means of transport, the party arrived at Fort Yukon July 15th, 1873. They found the Alaska Commercial Company's agent Moses Mercier there, and he extended them every consideration and assistance in his power. On the 21st, to the surprise of Harper and party, as he told me, Jack McQuesten and his friends, together with a pick-up they had made, one Nicholson, who had been in the Hudson's Bay employment, but left it and stayed with the Indians till he found McQuesten and party on the Peel, joined them. McQuesten tells me in his paper that Moses Mercier was in charge at Fort Yukon, and quaintly says, "He let us have fifty pounds of flour. It was all that he could spare. That was quite a treat to us, as that was the first we had had for two years."

At Yukon Harper met an Indian who had quite a chunk of native copper. Anxious inquiry elicited the information that it came from White River, more than four hundred miles up the Yukon. He decided to go in search of it, and two of his companions cast their lot with him, but Kansellar severed his connection with the party, and went down-river with McQuesten and associates. McQuesten's party went down about fifty miles and wintered in the vicinity of Goat Mountain. They killed five moose and two bears in the fall, and in the winter set their nets under

GOLD DISCOVERIES AND MINING

the ice in a near-by lake and caught all the white fish they could use. In the spring they returned to Fort Yukon by dog-team, having brought four with them from the Mackenzie. On May 10th the ice broke up and ran thickly for three days; on the 20th Harper and party joined them from up-river, and on June 4th Mercier, McQuesten and party, and Harper and party all started for St. Michael in Mercier's barge, arriving June 20th. François Mercier, Moses's brother, was in charge there, and he took McQuesten, Mayo, and Hart into the employ of the company. Harper and the others got provisions and returned on the steamer to the Tanana River, where they spent the season prospecting. The boat reached Yukon August 20th, and as good reports of furs had come from the region of the then "Tron Deg" (now the Klondike), McQuesten continued with the boat and established Fort Reliance, as has been detailed.

We will now return to Harper and his two associates at Yukon. After recuperating, and fixing their sorely mishandled boat, they started for White River. We may state here that this river was thus named by Robert Campbell because of the colour of the water. There are immense deposits of volcanic ash up it; which is in the form of an impalpable white powder, which is simply pulverized pumice-stone. In rainy weather this washes into the river in such quantities that the

H

water is actually thick with it and has a creamy white colour.

At the mouth of the stream they afterwards named Fortymile they found such good prospects that they were about to ascend it and test further, but some Indians camped there made them believe that there was a terribly dangerous cañon some distance up; a cañon impassable to them, and so dangerous they would likely all lose their lives if they attempted it. They could not afford to run any risk, so continued to the White. We may pause here and ask, If they had only known then, what they became well acquainted with not long after, that the Indian description was a gross exaggeration, and had gone up the Fortymile, what would the result have been? and how differently might the story of the Yukon have been written? In the nature of things it is certain that they would have anticipated the discovery of coarse gold by Franklin and Madison by thirteen years, and, as we will see later, the discovery of coarse gold led to a very marked change in the methods of mining, with vastly better results. Then, too, such a discovery at that time would have precipitated international questions at a time when neither side had very much interest in the frozen north, and the final adjustment might have been different from what it is. They continued to White River, which they reached in September, and after making their way up it as far as the falling water and swift current would let them, they prepared to winter. Their stock of flour had run down to three hundred pounds, one hundred per man, but they killed five moose in a few days, and looked with complacency on the approaching winter. McQuesten's narrative says that the party returned to the mouth of the river and built winter quarters, from which, when the rivers were covered with ice, they made a trip up the Stewart, about fifty miles, prospecting; but Harper's story was that they remained on the White River looking for the copper, which they did not find. This was small wonder, for copper found there was native copper lying in the drift of the creek and river bottoms, and being drift itself its parent lode might be leagues away. In the winter it would be all ice-covered, and the search fruitless for one ignorant of the conditions. It has since been found in abundance on the head of both the White and Tanana rivers, also on Copper River, flowing into the Pacific Ocean, all heading in the same plateau. It is highly improbable that they could have gathered the information they did about the river and its topography in a stay of only a few weeks. Harper told me they prospected at the mouth of the Stewart as they passed it, but the shortness of supplies prevented them thinking of aught else than getting to some place where they could renew their stores. Meat they could get in abundance, but a straight meat diet is very trying except for a short time. Then, too, they had been without information from the world and its doings for two years, and they yearned to learn what old mother earth had been worrying about while they were absent, so determined to get to some base of news supplies, and St. Michael being the easiest of approach, they struck for it.

While prospecting in the vicinity of the mouth of the Tanana an Indian showed Harper some small nuggets of gold, which he told him had been found on the side of a mountain visible from where they were. Harper sought assiduously for more at the place pointed out, but did not find any. Afterwards he learned that they had been brought from the upper Koyukuk River. Had he known this in time he no doubt would have gone in search of the field. In 1875 he made a trip down the Yukon from Reliance to where Eagle now is, and from there crossed to the north fork of the Fortymile, and followed it down to the main river, from where he crossed the divide between Fortymile and Sixtymile rivers. On the latter he found such good pay that he determined to try it the following summer, and sent out for a tank of quicksilver, but before it arrived, he had the trouble with the Indians we have referred to, which McQuesten settled by paying for the women. When the trouble was over, and the quicksilver came, he could not afford to give up

GOLD DISCOVERIES AND MINING

his employment with the company. Some time after this he made an exploratory trip to the head of the Tanana, going up Fortymile to reach it. He found good prospects, but never could afford to give up his business with the company and take to mining exclusively. At that time also the supplies brought to the country by the company were intended to meet the requirements of the fur trade, and mining being so desultory was never thought of, as requiring its own peculiar articles. In this way Harper, though well aware of a good deal of the country's potential worth, could not afford to begin the development of it himself, but his letters to friends on the outside helped to arouse curiosity and create interest. Thus this man who first thought of trying it as a mining field was compelled by circumstances to devote himself to something else. He lived in the region for twenty-four years, and after testing nearly every mining field that has since been found except the golden Klondike, over which he hunted while stationed at Reliance, gathering abundant stores of meat, but never dreaming of the richer stores beneath his feet, had to leave Dawson, in August, 1897, almost exhausted with tuberculosis, and died from it at Yuma, Arizona, in the following November, just as the Klondike was opening its golden gate to him. His confidence in the future of the country never flagged, and we cannot help feeling that fate was unkind to one who had come so near the achievement of wealth through hard toil, yet died when just past his prime, sixty-two, at a time when everything seemed most favourable for the realization of the hopes he had entertained throughout all the trying years of his waiting, watching, and struggling. His life friend and associate Fred Hart died about the same time, and their ashes lie far apart—at San Francisco and Dawson.

McQuesten, though never so actively connected with mining as Harper, was nevertheless in sympathy with it, and aided the craft all he could, by helping them with supplies and material, as much as lay in his power. Many a story is told in the Yukon, and by the old-timers wherever they are, of Jack's goodness of heart, and leniency in collecting accounts, and we cannot let the occasion pass without recalling one at least, typical of all the rest. A miner who had got an outfit on credit, to be paid for at next clean-up, came in to see Jack, intending no doubt to do the "square thing"; saw him, and after the usual "howdys" and "ho's," asked Jack how much he owed. Examination showed the balance against him to be slightly over seven hundred dollars. The information surprised the debtor into the exclamation—

"Seven hundred! H—l, Jack, I've only got five hundred, how'm I goin' to pay seven hundred with five?"

"Oh, that's all right, give us your five hundred,

FRED HART

GOLD DISCOVERIES AND MINING

and we'll credit you and let the rest stand till next clean-up."

"But, Jack, I want some more stuff. How'm I goin' to get that?"

"Why, we'll let you have it as we did before."

"But, d—n it, Jack, I haven't had a spree yet."

"Well, go and have your little spree, come back with what is left, and we'll credit you with it and go on as before."

Alas for human frailty, when he came from his spree there was nothing left, and kindly Jack let him have another outfit, increasing the indebtedness to about twelve hundred, to be paid for *next clean-up*, and so *ad infinitum*.

These recipients are to-day not the most appreciative of Jack. One resident of the northland, after the experience of several years had taught him that a disinclination to work does not generally conduce to the accumulation of this world's goods, reasoned, if the word can be applied to the kind, that the world owed him a living anyway, and as the only tangible representative of the world he could find in that region was the Alaska Commercial Company, it, of course, was responsible to him, and to it he would go. This he did, through kindly Jack, with such success that he owed it some four thousand dollars after four or five years of his distinguished patronage. At that time there was no way to compel him to pay, even if he had the means, and as he wanted to stand well with the community he put it publicly, that there must be justice somewhere, that the company had been swindling the United States in particular, and the public generally, in possessing such a monopoly in the seal fisheries of the Pribilof Islands. Justice must work in somewhere, and he decided that this was the place, in one instance at least. "Justice *we must have*, gentlemen, and I stand for it if no one else does," and strange to say some thought he was right. There is occasion for regret in the fact that this individual was one of the lucky ones in the Klondike strike, and also occasion for gratification that when the proper authority was inaugurated in the country he was compelled, being then able, to pay his debt. So the United States and the public are still unavenged!

CHAPTER VII

FIRST GOLD SENT OUT

THE first gold known to have come from any part of the Yukon basin to the outside world was sent to St. Michael in 1880 by George Holt, an employee of the Alaska Commercial Company. It consisted of two small nuggets, and he stated they were given to him by a Tanana River Indian, but just where they were found does not appear. Mr. Holt is also credited with having led the first party over the Dyea Pass and down the Yukon in 1875. Five years later another party, led by a Mr. Edward Bean, crossed the summit, but how far he went beyond is not known. Between 1882 and '83 it is said that a small number of nuggets were brought from the upper Yukon to San Francisco, but this appears to me doubtful, as no coarse gold was found there again till quite recently, and if such a discovery were once made it would hardly be allowed to lapse.

FIRST PROSPECTORS DOWN-RIVER

According to de Wolfe, before quoted, in 1882 a party of Arizona prospectors entered the upper Yukon and went down as far as the Stewart, up which three of them went, they said, two hundred miles, prospecting. If they attained this distance they would have reached the falls. At one or two places on this stream I saw where prospecting holes had been sunk in the gravel on the bank, which the age of the brushwood grown in them showed must have been dug about that time. They reported to Edward Schieffelin of Tombstone, Arizona, to whom we have already referred. The report mentioned the existence of gold, silver, nickel, copper, and coal, which showed that those gentlemen must have been exaggerating, as no nickel is known now, and as for coal, they might have noticed it at Fivefinger Rapids, but not likely anywhere else. Copper is found near White Horse, but miles away from the Yukon.

This statement is quoted from de Wolfe's paper, but his date must be wrong, for both he and McQuesten agree that Schieffelin came up the river from St. Michael in 1883. Now as conditions then were, Schieffelin would have to sail from the Pacific coast of the United States in August of 1882 to reach St. Michael that fall, as McQuesten says he did. He might possibly leave

ALASKA COMMERCIAL CO.'S WHARF, ST. MICHAEL, ALASKA, 1897

FIRST GOLD SENT OUT

a month later, but it is very unlikely. Then, too, it is not probable that any party would try to traverse Dyea Pass until June, as Lake Labarge seldom opens to navigation till the eighth or tenth of that month; from that date till August 1st would give the party a very short time in which to make such an extensive exploration, and they would have to start on the return trip at that date if they expected to report to Schieffelin in time to let him get away to St. Michael. There are other hindrances to mention that would put the question beyond a doubt, but I think I am safe in saying that the prospectors made their exploration in 1881 if they made it at all. Silver has been found up the Windy Arm part of Tagish Lake, at a place so far out of the direct line of travel that they were not likely to have gone there.

McQuesten says Schieffelin and party went up the Yukon from St. Michael in the fall of 1882 to Tanana Station, where they wintered. The next spring they prospected in the vicinity, and found coarse gold in a gulch called Maybeso Gulch, but it did not pay, and in the fall the party all left the country, except a man named Phillip Fancio. De Wolfe says Schieffelin was in search of quartz lodes, and was not interested in placer-digging.

In the summer of 1883 four men—Richard Poplin, Charles McConkey, Benjamin Beach, and C. Marks—went over the Dyea Pass and down the

Yukon, prospecting as they went, and when they reached the Stewart went up it to the McQuesten. By this time they had to make for Fort Reliance, as their supplies were running out, and when they reached there it was found the steamer had broken down on the lower river, and they had to continue to Tanana, where they wintered. In the spring McQuesten took them up on the boat, and they spent the summer prospecting on the Stewart. In the fall they all went out over the Dyea Pass, so they could not, at most, have put in more than three months' prospecting. On the way up the Yukon they met Thomas Boswell and Franklin, who were mining on the upper river, working on the banks and bars. Poplin and party told Boswell that he could find plenty of better digging on the Stewart. Boswell and party took the hint, and went down to Reliance, where they remained through the winter. In the month of April they sleighed up to the Stewart, hauling the sleds themselves, the custom then, and prospected the river as they went, by building fires on the bars, thawing the gravel and washing it. They marked the bars that would pay as they determined them in this way, but striking Chapman's Bar, about ninety miles up, they found it so good that they determined to work it for the summer. The average per man for the season was about one hundred dollars per day, which, with rockers to wash it with, was considered extraordinary. Richard Poplin returned the same spring from Juneau with Peter Wybourg, Francis Morphat, and Jeremiah Bertrand, and went up the Stewart, passing Boswell and party at Chapman's Bar. They continued to what was afterward named Steamboat Bar, about seven miles farther up, and settled to work. Their clean-up for the season was about thirty-five thousand dollars. They went into camp in September, about twenty-five miles from the mouth of the river.

News of this success on the Stewart reached the outside, and in the summer of 1886 about one hundred men came in and worked on the river. They were scattered in their arrival, and also in their position on the river; still, in spite of this handicap, they averaged about one thousand dollars each. Anticipating from the success of Boswell and party, and Poplin and party in 1885, a big rush, Harper and McQuesten arranged to establish a supply post at the mouth of the river in the summer of 1886, which was done, and the Stewart was looked on as the camp for some time to come. Later on, in the remarks on mining methods, we will see how slow and crude the work here was, and how rich the gravel must have been to yield as it did. As we have seen, the Stewart River was pretty well prospected up to the falls, and the McQuesten to an unknown distance. On the Stewart all the good ground is on a stretch of ninety-five miles, beginning at a point about fifteen miles above the mouth, and extending about the same distance above the mouth of the McQuesten. No one appears to have found anything above the last point, either at that time or since. Above the falls not much prospecting has yet been done, but reports speak well of the surface showings.

On the McQuesten no one in those early days found anything to rank with the bars on the Stewart, consequently nothing of note was done on it. Recently, on some of its affluents along its upper reaches, coarse gold has been found in areas that promise well for its future, but as the stream is not navigable for steamers, and difficult for small boats, it is very much handicapped.

In the summer of 1882 twelve men came over the divide, as it was then termed, that is, over the Dyea Pass, and wintered at Fort Reliance. Among them was Joseph Ladue, who afterwards became identified with the development of the country, and William Moore, who piloted the steamer *Arctic*. They prospected during the summer of 1883 on Fortymile and Sixtymile rivers, but did not strike anything of note, and all left in the fall except Ladue and one other. I mention this to show how uncertain prospecting is, for both those rivers became famous camps afterward.

The rivers Fortymile and Sixtymile were so named because they were estimated to be

FIRST GOLD SENT OUT

those distances respectively from Fort Reliance. Seventymile River, below Egbert, was named for the same reason.

In 1886 Franklin and Henry Madison made an examination of the Stewart to the falls, and the McQuesten as far as they could ascend in their boats. They appear to have been prejudiced against both streams, for Franklin remarked to the miners on the river that he did not like the kind of trees that grew on the bars, and that gold was never found where wild onions or leeks grew, of which there is abundance along the shores of that stream. Being firm in their convictions, they went down-stream to the Fortymile, which they ascended, and very soon made the discovery of coarse gold on bed-rock, up that stream about twenty-three miles from its mouth, just past where the International Boundary crosses it. They returned to Stewart Post in October, proclaiming, according to the code of the country, the discovery. This was the first coarse gold discovery in the region, and as coarse gold is the great desideratum of all miners, it made great excitement in the territory. After Franklin and Madison left the Stewart two brothers named Day came along, and made over thirty dollars per day on one of the bars which Franklin and Madison rejected.

The Fortymile discovery upset all the calculations with regard to the Stewart, as every one decided to strike for the new field, and the camp being practically deserted in the spring of 1887, Harper and McQuesten had to move to the new ground. They built a new post at the mouth of the Fortymile, which they were just beginning when I arrived there September 9th, 1887. It is estimated that there were two hundred thousand dollars taken out that season. As there was no base of supplies above Fortymile nearly all the work and prospecting done in the country had to be done near Fortymile; consequently, we find that all the discoveries made for some years were confined to the Fortymile region. For several years from that date about three hundred men mined in the region, but as the small steamer plying on the river could not bring provisions enough to winter more than one hundred in the country, the other two hundred had to make their way out, some up the river by poling their boats, very hard, difficult work, and some down to St. Michael on the chance of catching a United States Revenue cutter home bound, or the Alaska Commercial Company steamer to San Francisco. After the *Arctic* began to make regular trips on the river from St. Michael, in 1890, there were plenty of provisions in the country as a rule, and more men wintered there, and prospecting was done in the winter months. It is hardly necessary to say how many branches of the

FIRST GOLD SENT OUT

Fortymile were discovered, and give their names. We will close this record by mentioning the discovery of gold on the tributaries of Sixtymile, two of which, Miller and Glacier Creeks, especially the former, were famous, until eclipsed by the Klondike discovery.

As we have already stated, McQuesten sent two men, whom he names Syrosca and Pitka, both native Indians, to prospect on the head of Birch Creek, which takes its rise close to the Tanana, and flows into the Yukon about forty miles below Fort Yukon. In its course it runs parallel to the Yukon River for nearly one hundred miles, and at Circle City is only some seven or eight miles from it. McQuesten says that on his way up-river in September, 1894, he found about seventy-five miners waiting for the boat. They had laid off a town-site, and had about thirty cabins under construction. In that and the following season, nine paying creeks were discovered, Dead Wood (or Mastedon), Eagle, Hogan, Harrison, Independent, Miller, Boulder, Greenhorn, and Yankee. The entire clean-up in 1895 was about four hundred thousand dollars.

Fortymile and Circle City divided the attention of most of the miners till 1896, when the Klondike was discovered. A few prospected on the Koyukuk with such success that a small steamer was put on the stream. Others prospected along the watershed between the Yukon River and Arctic

Ocean, with varied success, but some of the reports point to important discoveries in the future. Prospecting in that region is greatly handicapped by nature, and at present by lack of transport facilities at the places where they are most needed.

CHAPTER VIII

DISCOVERY OF THE KLONDIKE

IN August, 1896, the world-startling discovery of the Klondike was made, which for a year or two put a period to all exploration and prospecting except in its immediate vicinity.

We will introduce an account of this discovery by referring to the name of the river from which the field takes its name. We may recall the reader's attention to the fact that we have previously referred to the name "Tron Deg" being given this stream by Harper and McQuesten. They got the name from the Indians in the vicinity, and, being short and easily pronounced, they adopted it. The natives in that and most other countries name places and things after some prominent characteristic or feature, and in most cases the names so given are compound words, long and difficult to pronounce except for those given to the study of philology, which but few miners or traders are. This accounts for so few of the native names being recorded, much less retained, and is the reason for the name Fortymile and others, instead of the Indian name which signifies the river, or rather water, the word literally is, that flows swiftly past the stones, which is long and difficult to pronounce, there being a great many guttural and nasal sounds in the language. Now, while I did not devote much time to the study of the language, I always did, when opportunity offered through some native who understood enough English and was intelligent enough to comprehend my object, try to get the correct native names of places and things, and their correct pronunciation, and note the words composing them, with their meaning in English. I can, therefore, appreciate the difficulty such a task presents to the ordinary miner or trader, for often it was only after several attempts that I was able definitely to fix the sound. For illustration, the Indian word for water, on the upper half of the Yukon and on nearly all the Mackenzie, is "duh" or "tuh," but so pronounced through the throat and nose, as I heard it, that it is difficult to say exactly which sound is intended; in fact, in pronouncing it, I have used both without criticism. In compounding a name for a stream the word for water is always terminal, as, for example, the Hootalinque, the Indian name of which is "Teslin-tuh" or "duh," meaning "Teslin-water." The word "Teslin" is the native name of a large fish found in the lake out of which this stream flows. As I gathered from the natives I talked to, they employ what might be termed a diminutive of the word " tuh " or " duh," when the stream or water is small, and this takes the form " tiuck " or " diuck," but generally pronounced so fast and indistinctly that it sounds like " tick " or " dick," and some so pronounce it that one might call it " tig " or " dig." I spent hours talking to all the Indians in the vicinity, whom I could make understand me, to get the correct pronunciation, and I think I succeeded. This being true, the correct native name for the Klondike is " Trondiuck," or " tiuck." This in English means the " Hammer-water," from the fact that this stream was a famous salmon-run, and barriers of stakes were driven across the mouth to compel the fish to enter the traps set for them. These stakes had to be driven or " hammered " into the gravel in the riverbed, hence the name. When I passed the mouth, September 1st, 1887, the whole width of the river-bed was staked, and half a dozen families were camped on an island in the mouth of the Klondike, which has since become a bar, the timber being washed away. How the name Klondike came to be adopted is incomprehensible to me, for to the old-timers who had occasion to name it, it was "Tron-deg," and the present name does not resemble that more than it does the native name "Tron-diuck." The word was pronounced to me as if one started to say "duck," but put in a slurred "i" before "u." We must admit that Klondike is easier to say, and more euphonic. A word in very common use in the territory, which has found its way out, and is sometimes quoted in a slangy way, is "mush." Its origin is not so difficult to trace, for it is simply a corruption of the French word "marche," which the dog-drivers on the Mackenzie used as a word of command to their dogs to go on. The Indian corrupted it to "mash," and the average resident of the Yukon, with his or her proclivity to miscall things, changed it to "mush." Had they known that it is the word used by the commanding officer of troops, when he orders his command to proceed, march, they might have got it right, but that is doubtful; "mush" is original, and slang, and there you are.

Leading up to the discovery of the Klondike, that all credit may rest where it is due, we have to go back of the date a year or two.

We have already referred to the advent to the country, in 1882, of Joe Ladue, of French-Canadian descent, born in New York State. Failing in his mining expectations, he entered the service of Harper and McQuesten, and when they separated in 1889 he continued his connection with Harper as a partner in business. His residence in the country, with its trying winter journeys, and lack of even the most ordinary household comforts in the pioneer days, wrecked

DISCOVERY OF THE KLONDIKE   119

his constitution, and, like his partner and friend Harper, he became a victim to consumption a few years after fortune opened its gates to him in the discovery of the Klondike. He was a most enthusiastic advocate of the Yukon and its possibilities, which sometimes led him into awkward situations, for every reported new strike was just what they had been looking for, a veritable El Dorado, and every one was going to become rich now and for ever. It takes such enthusiasm to sustain a man in such a country, and happy is he who is ultimately rewarded by having his visions realized. Joe was for some time in charge of the new trading-post at Ogilvie, where all the incoming miners called on their way down the river, and he never failed to encourage them with tales of wonderful prospects at newly found places.

Among those who came to the Yukon seeking adventure, before the Klondike discovery, was Robert Henderson, from Big Island, off the north coast of Nova Scotia. He had been a sailor for some years, and in that capacity had been pretty well over the globe. Of an adventurous nature, he took to hunting for gold, not so much to become rich as to find adventure, for those who know him best do not believe he would work the richest claim on earth if he had to stay on it till it was worked out. So constituted we find him in all his sojourn in the Yukon, and he is there now, continually looking for new fields. So, when others were tramping over the Fortymile and Birch Creek regions, "Bob" was in another quarter.

In July, 1894, Henderson and two associates, Kendrick and Snider, arrived at Ogilvie, where they found the ever-smiling Joe Ladue in charge. He was ready for them with a good story about the prospects on Indian River, which joined the Yukon nearly twenty miles below them. It was comparatively virgin ground, and that was enough for "Bob" Henderson. His associates, however, were not so easily enthused, and went back to Colorado, whence they had all come only a few weeks before. Indian River is parallel in its course with the Klondike, and as the distance between them in an air line is only fifteen to twenty miles, the watershed between them is sharp in its slopes, and so well adapted to catch and hold the gold contained in its gravels as they are gradually worked lower and lower by the rushing waters.

After a few days' stay at Ogilvie, Henderson and a new-found comrade started for Indian River, and went up as far as a creek they named Quartz, and continued up it to the divide between it and what is now Hunker Creek. Provisions ran out, and they came down the Indian on the ice in October, but found the Yukon still open. This must have been a novel experience for a man

JOE LADUES' HOUSE AT OGILVIE, 1895

who had been a great deal in the tropics, and had spent the most of fourteen years in Colorado before coming here. After a rest, and renewal of his outfit, Henderson went back alone to Indian River, and spent the winter of 1894-5 in prospecting, mainly on Quartz Creek. He had to thaw his prospect holes down to bed-rock, which to a lone man was laborious and tedious work. We are sorry to have to record that he found a few colours only in each of the holes. It is interesting to note that this creek, in the days of the Klondike rush, was boomed for awhile, but fell flat after a season; notwithstanding this, it is now considered a fairly good creek with, if not high-grade dirt, plenty of paying stuff. This is due, more than anything else, to the improvement in methods, and cheapening in processes.

In March he started up the river to prospect a large branch, named Australia Creek. He had to make so many trips back and forth with his outfit and supplies that he was sixty days reaching his objective point. He found nothing to encourage him, and moose and caribou being plentiful he killed some, made a boat of their skins, floated down the Indian, and paddled up the Yukon to Ogilvie. As he was prospecting these upper creeks an accident happened to him that might have ended his career, and, as he was alone, if it had done so it is improbable that he would ever have been seen again, or any certain idea formed of what had become of him. In prospecting on the head of Australia Creek it became necessary for him to cross, and as it was at flood-tide with the spring freshets, he had to fell a tree over it. In order to make it passable the numerous limbs had to be cut off, and to do this he steadied himself with a stick, held in his left hand, which rested on the bottom of the creek. While cutting limbs the stick broke, and losing his balance, he fell in such a way that the sharp point of one of the limbs just got caught in the calf of his left leg, piercing it in such a way that he hung suspended from the limb until his sailor craft enabled him to swing himself up and on to the tree, taking care to keep hold of his axe, the only one he had. The wound confined him to his camp for fourteen days. The only diversion he had during his confinement was to watch the numerous wild animals that came around the camp. He appeared to be as much an object of curiosity to them as they were to him. After his wound had healed sufficiently to allow of his departure, he embarked in his skin boat and drifted down to the mouth of Quartz Creek, up which he went a day and a half, where he put up a dam to raise water for sluicing. He worked sixteen days on this, and at its completion sluiced a day and a half, cleaning up thirteen dollars. Discouraged by this and the wound in his leg, he again embarked in his skin boat, drifted down the Indian, and poled up the Yukon River to Ogilvie, where he obtained a fresh supply of provisions and a companion, one William Redford. They made their way back to Quartz Creek, where they ground-sluiced some of the top material off in preparation for next season's operations. Their provisions were then exhausted, and they returned to Ogilvie, where, after waiting for several weeks, Henderson was able to obtain a year's supply of the staple articles of the country: bacon, flour, beans, tea, coffee, sugar, and a very little butter. With these he returned alone to Quartz Creek, where he spent the winter prospecting, burning holes to bed-rock, and other work preparatory to a big clean-up the following spring. He killed two moose for winter meat, but though he cached the meat securely, as he thought, the wolves got it and did not leave him a taste. In the early spring another pioneer, Al. Day, a French-Canadian, and a companion came up to see him and found him sluicing. He had already taken out four hundred dollars, but they returned at once, lest the track they had made on the river should overflow. Henderson cleaned up altogether six hundred and twenty dollars. The amount was not encouraging, though one might think it not bad for a sailor who had never before mined in a frozen country in his life. He then ascended Australia Creek, which he prospected over all its length, taking in its branches as he did so. Nothing satisfactory was found, as might naturally be anticipated from such a cursory examination, and he drifted back to Quartz, and ascended it to the head, from which he crossed a watershed to a stream which he surmised flowed into the Klondike. This he called Gold Bottom. Here he found a two-cent prospect, that is, two cents of gold to a pan. This was something better than he had heretofore found, and he determined to work it. He went to Ogilvie to replenish his rations and try and induce some one to come with him and relieve the loneliness. He got the needed supplies, and was fortunate enough to induce two Swedes, Munson and Swanson, Dalton, nationality unknown, and an Italian, Liberati, to accompany him. The return trip was made by the Indian River and up Quartz Creek. Meanwhile Joe Ladue was spreading the news of the new discovery as much as opportunity offered, and many prospectors and new-comers went in search of the new field. About the end of July food again ran out, and Henderson returned alone to Ogilvie for more. Going down the Indian he found the water so low that his empty boat often grounded, and he knew that it would be impossible to return that way with a load. Believing as he did that he was working on a tributary of the Tron-deg (Klondike), he determined to go down the Yukon to the mouth of that stream to the camp. He had,

DISCOVERY OF THE KLONDIKE

of course, to assume that the creek he was working on joined the main stream quite a distance above the mouth, and could only guess when he came to the right one.

At the mouth of the Klondike he saw George Washington Carmac, whom story has connected prominently with the discovery of the Klondike, and some think the discovery of the Yukon itself. Henderson, in accordance with the unwritten miners' code, told Carmac of the discovery he had made on Gold Bottom, and invited him to come up and stake. Carmac was then engaged in salmon-fishing with his Indian friends and associates, the male members of whom were Skookum, or "strong" Jim, and Tagish (sometimes Cultus, or "no good") Charlie. As Henderson tells the story Carmac promised to take it in, and take his Indian associates with him, but to this Henderson strongly objected, saying he did not want his creek to be staked by a lot of natives, more especially natives from the upper river. Carmac seemed to be offended by the objection, so they parted. I have this story substantially the same from both Henderson and Carmac, the latter, of course, laying a little stress on the objection to the Indians. I have had long interviews with both Jim and Charlie, and some of the others camped with them on the Klondike at that time, and reduced the purport of our talks to writing. As I have said, both Henderson and Carmac gave me the same story about Henderson having told Carmac of the new discovery, and the Indians assured me that they knew "Bob," as they call Henderson, told George, as they called Carmac, of it and asked him to go and stake on it; that much, therefore, may be assumed without doubt. The stories told me by the Indians may be questioned, but they were very sincere in their tone and assertions when telling me. I took the precaution to interview them separately and afterwards get them all together and criticize and discuss the narrative of each in committee of the whole, as we might term it. Put in as concise terms as I can frame it, Jim's story tells us that he, Charlie, and George were, as we know, camped at the mouth of the Klondike fishing, but as a straight fish diet becomes monotonous in time, in order to procure some variety it was agreed that they would get out some saw logs, take them down to Fortymile, and sell them to the saw-mill there. The current rate was twenty-five dollars per thousand feet board measure. Much depended on Jim in this work, and he did a good deal of examination in the woods around the place to find the best and most convenient logs. This work took him some distance up a creek afterwards known as Bonanza, which joins the Klondike less than a mile above the mouth. He informed me he found some very good logs up this creek at various places, and in order to learn whether or not they could be

ROBERT HENDERSON

DISCOVERY OF THE KLONDIKE

floated down to the Yukon, he had to make a close examination of the creek bed. In doing this he said he found some colours of gold at various places in the gravel, and particularly at where claim sixty-six below discovery was afterwards located he found what he considered very fair prospects. He told the fishing-camp of this find, but it did not arouse much interest. Jim, according to his own story, was anxious to further investigate, but as George was chief councillor in the camp and did not appear much interested in the matter it was allowed to drop temporarily.

About twenty days after Henderson called at the camp, George told him to get ready for a tramp to find Bob. Jim, Charlie, and George started up Bonanza on the quest, with a gold pan, spade, axe, and such other tools as were necessary for a prolonged stay from camp, and such provisions as their means afforded, and according to the Indians the supply was not extensive nor diversified, being mostly fish. Travelling up the valley of Bonanza through the thick underbrush at that season was tedious and fatiguing, and the mosquito-laden atmosphere added torment to fatigue. A short distance below where they afterwards made discovery, both Jim and Charlie told me they, while panning during a rest, found a ten-cent pan. There is a slight discrepancy; each claimed that he made the find, but when confronted, it settled down to the mutually satisfactory statement that while resting they thought they would pan for fun. Jim took the pan and washed such dirt as Charlie gathered for him, so they both found it, though neither expected it. This discovery caused a ripple of excitement in the community, small as it was, and it was decided that if the Gold Bottom trials failed they would devote further attention to this place. The Indians both told me they asked George if they would tell Bob of this find, and that George directed them to say nothing about it till they came back, if they did, and investigated further, then if they found anything good they might tell.

Travelling was so tiresome and tedious in the valley that, when they came to the confluence with the creek now called Eldorado, they took to the divide between it and Bonanza, and followed the crest of this divide around the head of Bonanza Creek, where, finding the marks made by Henderson, they descended to him. Arrived there they were nearly bare of provisions, and completely out of tobacco, a serious predicament for Jim and Charlie. Henderson, either through shortage himself or dislike of the Indians, or both, would not let them have anything, though Jim and Charlie both assured me they offered to pay well for all they could get, which Jim was both able and willing to do. As they did not find any prospect approaching in value the ten-cent pan on Bonanza, they remained a very short time

DISCOVERY OF THE KLONDIKE

at Henderson's camp, and made their way back to the head of the creek which first gave fame to the Klondike-Bonanza. Before they got far down it their provisions were entirely exhausted, and as they prospected on the way down, and Jim was hunting for meat, their progress was slow; and their hunger was becoming acute, with exhaustion and weakness fast following. To shorten the story of Jim and Charlie, for they dwelt long on this part of the narrative, Jim at last, when they were all too tired and weak to do further prospecting, got a moose. He had fired at one before, but missed; the first time in his life he assured me, and he had a good rifle too, Winchester, he exclaimed proudly.

After killing the moose, Jim says he called on the others, whom he had left some distance away, to come to him. While waiting for them to come he looked in the sand of the creek where he had gone to get a drink, taking with him a bit of the moose. He found gold, he said, in greater quantities than he had ever seen it before. When the others joined him the moose meat was cooked, and they had a feed. Then he showed them the gold in the sand. They remained two days at this place panning, and testing the gravel up and down the creek in the vicinity. After satisfying themselves that they had the best spot, and deciding to stake and record there, they got into a dispute as to who should stake discovery claim,

Jim claiming it by right of discovery, and Carmac claiming it, Jim says, on the ground that an Indian would not be allowed to record it. Jim says the difficulty was finally settled by agreeing that Carmac was to stake and to record discovery claim, and assign half of it, or a half-interest in it, to Jim, so on the morning of August 17th, 1896, Carmac staked discovery claim five hundred feet in length up and down the direction of the creek valley, and No. 1 below discovery of the same length; both the full width of the valley bottom, or from base to base of the hill on either side, as the regulations then read. No. 2 below was staked for Tagish Charlie, and No. 1 above for Skookum Jim. The gold they panned out of the surface gravel on discovery was put into a Winchester rifle cartridge shell and the party went to camp at the mouth of the Klondike. There a small raft of saw logs was prepared for the saw-mill at Fortymile. Carmac and Charlie went down on it, and Jim was sent back to the claim to watch it, as the country all around there was alive with men looking for the Henderson discovery. In proof of this I have only to quote from my notes to show that two days after Carmac and party staked, that is, August 19th, 1896, Edward Monahan and Greg Stewart staked two claims that subsequently were found to be Nos. 28 and 29, below discovery about three miles, and the following day D. Edwards, J. Moffat, D. Robertson, and C. Kimball staked

DISCOVERY OF THE KLONDIKE

what proved on continuous survey to be Nos. 16, 17, 18, and 19 below discovery. An event which led to a great deal of misunderstanding and trouble, which will be fully related later, transpired on August 22nd, that is, what was called a miners' meeting was held on the hillside opposite to claim No. 17 below discovery. Twenty-five men were present, and there must have been nearly as many more wandering about the valley looking for Henderson's discovery. Now as we have seen, Carmac, Jim, and Charlie left discovery claim in the forenoon of the 17th, and as that is at least eleven miles from the mouth of the Klondike, consequently a good day's tramp through the woods and swamps of the region, and they did not reach the Yukon till that evening, if they reached it that day at all, we are positive they could not give any notice on the Yukon River of the new discovery till the 18th. As they had to gather the logs for the raft they took to Fortymile, and it took a long day to float down, they could not possibly reach there, the main camp of the district at the time, till the 21st, so we can feel assured that the men who staked on the 19th and 20th, and those who attended the meeting on the 22nd, could not all owe their information to Carmac and his associates, and he can hardly be properly credited with the discovery of the Klondike. Henderson has always bitterly resented Carmac's neglect to send him word of the new discovery as he—Henderson—says Carmac promised he would do, if he found anything better than where they were working on Gold Bottom. The result to Henderson was that he did not learn of the new discovery which was brought about through his labours and invitation to come to Gold Bottom till after all the ground on both Bonanza and Eldorado was staked. Henderson could not, owing to short season and falling water, lose the time to go to the office at Fortymile and record his claim on Gold Bottom, until after Andrew Hunker had located on the creek below him, and had gone down to Fortymile, and not only recorded a discovery claim, but had the creek named after him, notwithstanding that Henderson had marked a large tree at the junction of this creek with the Klondike when he left his boat there on his way up in July, " This creek to be known as Gold Bottom Creek." As the mining regulations then were, only one discovery was allowed in " a district," the boundaries of which were fixed by the Government Agent. A discovery was allowed on Bonanza Creek to Carmac, and another on Gold Bottom, or as it was misnamed Hunker, to Hunker, and no more would be allowed in the Klondike district. The result was Henderson, after his two years' hard work, and his proclaiming his find and inviting every one he met at all interested in mining, and some he knew were not, to try the new field, got only an ordinary claim in it.

DISCOVERY OF THE KLONDIKE 133

When Carmac and Tagish Charlie reached Fortymile and related the new discovery not many paid much attention to it at first. Carmac had never followed mining as a business heretofore, though he had prospected some, and as he had just recently come to Fortymile and was not very well known, there was not that importance attached to his statements which might have been had he been a longer resident, and had he followed mining as a business. Also his association with the Indians for so long had created a prejudice against him in the community. When I first entered the country in 1887 I found him at Dyea Pass. He was then closely associated with the Tagish, or Stick Indians, as they were called. It was understood between these and the Chilcoot and Chilcat, or coast, Indians that the country north of the summit of the pass belonged to the Sticks, and all the coast to the south of it to the coast tribes. Carmac spoke both languages in a limited way, and had considerable influence with the Sticks. I employed him to help me over the pass and through his influence got a good deal of assistance from his Indian friends. Skookum Jim and Tagish Charlie were both there, and packed for me. Skookum well earned his sobriquet of "Skookum" or "strong," for he carried one hundred and fifty-six (156) pounds of bacon over the pass for me at a single trip. This might be considered a heavy load anywhere on any roads, but over the stony moraine of a glacier, as the first half of the distance is, and then up a steep pass, climbing more than three thousand feet in six or seven miles, some of it so steep that the hands have to be used to assist one up, certainly is a stiff test of strength and endurance. After we crossed the summit and while building our boat I employed Jim in various capacities, and always found him reliable, truthful, and competent to do any work I gave him. Afterwards, while working on his claim on Bonanza, I had more experience with him, and it only corroborated the opinion I have expressed of his character. Charlie I did not know so well. Poor Charlie, while celebrating during the holiday season last winter, fell off the railway bridge at Carcross on the White Pass Railway and was drowned. I had seen him last summer, and had quite a long chat with him about the old days, and the discovery journey to Henderson. Again on my way out last fall I had a lengthy interview with Jim, Charlie, and all the rest of the tribe at Carcross. The old days were gone over, and the old tales told, I am pleased to say with very little variation from the first version I heard of them.

SKOOKUM JIM

Jim is an enthusiast on prospecting, and his object in life now, apparently, is to make another big discovery that will be all his own. He is

NEAR THE BOUNDARY. ONE HALF OF THE PREVIOUS DAY'S BAG

particularly anxious to discover a big quartz lode, and fully realizes the importance to the country of such an accomplishment. He possesses a practical knowledge of prospecting that is far beyond what one would expect to find in an uneducated savage. Further, he is qualified as a prospector in a way that but few white men are, for he carries nothing on his outings, which last weeks at a time, but a rifle, hatchet, and gold pan. His food he shoots, and his hatchet is responsible for his shelter. He spent some time with me in consultation about a prospecting journey from Carcross over the divide between Tagish Lake and the Teslin River, and from there across country to the Pelly, McMillan, and Stewart. We discussed at length all the information we had both of the route and the best way to go about the work. He was waiting the fall of a little more snow to enable him to make way with his sled, which he intended to haul himself. There is something unusual in a man planning an expedition of this kind, it might be said alone, for though an old white man intended to accompany him, Jim would have to bear most of the burden. He was taking very little with him, trusting to his implements for all he wanted. The trip would occupy most of the winter, under the most favourable circumstances, but if something good was found early in the season he would return at once to proclaim it and record title to what was staked.

I might say much more in relation to the discovery of the Klondike, and the impression prevailing at the time Carmac and Charlie came down to Fortymile to proclaim it, leaving Jim to guard the claims staked, but it would only be an elaboration of what has already been stated.

CHAPTER IX

MR. OGILVIE'S VISIT TO THE COUNTRY IN 1887-8
AND OBSERVATIONS MADE THEN

WE will now go back to the time I first visited the territory in order to bring the record of the region, in lines other than mining, up to the discovery of the Klondike, which being responsible in a large measure for the settlement of the territory, and the discovery of later fields, may be called the summit of history in the district. I do not mean to imply that there will be no further story to tell, but now that the Yukon is connected with the outside by boat, rail, and wire there can never be the same romance, the same tragedy as in the days of 1896, '97, and '98. That there will be new finds there is no doubt, but the field will be filled so quickly that future Klondike excitements cannot last more than a few weeks, certainly not more than a few months at the most.

During the winter of 1887-8, many miners called at our winter quarters near the boundary. Knowing that I was in Government employ, and in a measure the Government representative in the district, all were eager to learn from me as much as possible what the intentions of the Government were with regard to the region. At that time, as the Dominion Government had no mines of any importance under its jurisdiction, the mining regulations were in a very embryonic state. Such as we had were based principally on the British Columbia mining laws, and were ill-suited indeed to a region where eternal frost could be found almost anywhere a foot or so beneath the surface. All placer claims were then limited to one hundred feet square. Up to the year 1887, all mining done in the territory was on the bars and banks of the streams, and most of this was known as skim diggings, that is, only the two to four feet of the surface was worked. This was because, in the great majority of cases, below that depth water was encountered, which prevented profitable work. In the banks, too, frost was often met before the work extended far. In view of these natural handicaps the regulation size of claim was unanimously considered much too small. Out of the hundred or so miners wintering in the country I must have met at least half, and talked over at considerable length all the matters pertaining to mining in the territory. All the views presented to me were embodied in quite a lengthy memorandum which I left with Harper and McQuesten to be forwarded to Ottawa at the first opportunity. In this way it was probable it would reach the Department of

OGILVIE'S PARTY ON THE YUKON, CARRYING IN TWO YEARS' PROVISIONS, 1887

MR. OGILVIE'S VISIT TO THE COUNTRY

the Interior late in August, whereas I was not likely, if I carried out my programme, to be there before November. This memorandum in the main endorsed the miners' views, and asked for amendments in the mining regulations to legalize them. It was asked that the size of creek claims be extended to at least three hundred feet in length measured in the direction of the valley, and run in width across the valley bottom, or from base to base of the hills on either side, as it was worded in the changed regulations.

The minimum length was fixed at three hundred feet, but five hundred was suggested as more suited to the peculiar conditions of the region. Another provision of the old regulations that was universally condemned was the tax or royalty of two per cent of the clean-up on each and every claim. As was quite natural, there was a very wide diversity of view among the miners on every subject discussed, and the more experienced ones seemed to differ more widely than the novices. Had a code agreeable to all been required, there never would have been one outlined, and the best I could do was to hear as patiently as possible the views of all. Many questions of engineering were placed before me for consideration and practical solution. One important feature was brought forth at almost every meeting with any one; the question of bed-rock mining, as in more favoured regions farther south. The frost was considered by many an insuperable barrier, and it was pretty generally believed that bed-rock could not be reached by any practicable method. It was assumed that here, as elsewhere, the best pay would be found at the lowest depths, but how to get through twenty, thirty, and forty or more feet of frozen sand, clay, and gravel at reasonable expenditure of time and money was the question, and as it developed it *was a burning question*. All sorts of ideas were propounded and discussed, many impracticable from the paraphernalia required, and some impossible of execution; still, all helped the discussion along. As I had seen holes burned in the frozen crusts of the streets in Ottawa to reach defective gas and waterpipes, and I had several times had to use the process myself for other purposes, I suggested this as I had seen it applied, substituting, of course, the wood of the country for the coke used in the city. As some of the miners had already used the firing method to secure the bar gravels uncovered by the very low water of the winter months, I used this as an argument in favour of burning down. Whether my advocacy had much, or little, or anything at all to do with the inception of the method I cannot say, but it was tried, and a tremendous impetus was given to mining in the region. Bed-rock was reached, and a quality and quantity of gold found that had not been dreamed of before.

The use of wood for burning involved provisions in the regulations for its acquisition. The preparation of the memorandum sent out was a serious bit of work for me. I wanted all that was worthy of note to reach the Department, whether I reached it or not, for there was some doubt expressed by the Indians as to whether or not we should succeed in reaching the Mackenzie by the way I proposed to go, and while I believed no action would be taken till I returned to headquarters, I wanted to ensure against my failure to do so, and so made the paper more complete than I should have done had there been no doubt about my reaching home.

In the early morning of March 17th, 1888, I bade good-bye to the last miners I saw at the mouth of Seventymile River, and started on my way to the mouth of the Mackenzie. I did this with regret, for my intercourse with the miners had been most pleasant, and my association with Harper and McQuesten most satisfactory, yet I left with a feeling of exultation that I was now on the return stretch of my long journey, though more than twenty-five hundred miles lay between me and the nearest railroad station, nearly all of which had to be surmounted by foot and paddle. I agreed with the miners to send them back by some of the Indians, who accompanied us part way, my impressions of the new route as a goldfield. I had to tell them that, a short distance from the Yukon on the stream I went up, the geological character of the country gave very little hope of any metal of value being found in it. I learned afterward that, notwithstanding my advice, some of them followed my track about twenty miles and prospected, but found nothing.

When I reached Ottawa in the following January, the then Deputy Minister of the Interior, the late A. M. Burgess, was most anxious to get all possible information about the country, as was the Minister, Mr. Dewdney, but most of my business was with Mr. Burgess. He had decided, before taking any action in connection with the territory, to await my arrival home. The condition of the country as I knew it was gone over very thoroughly, and with the memorandum I had sent out in the winter before us, we discussed very fully what was deemed best to do in the interest of the Canadian part of the territory. Mr. Burgess was very frank in asking me to place my views fully before him, and I was asked to say freely and fully what I thought had best be done at that time. I told him that our mining regulations, as far as known, were unfavourably commented on in comparison with those of the United States, where each mining community elected its own recorders, regulated the size of its claims, and did nearly everything else the majority of the miners thought wise, so long as they did not clash with the general mining law of the United States. I advised him that while Fortymile seemed to possess the essentials for a pretty stable camp, most of the diggings on it were on the American side of the boundary, that at the time there were not freighting facilities enough to support more than one small camp, and that until such times as there were more and better means of transport it would be unwise in us to interfere with the affairs of the region, for the reason that most of the miners, while of foreign origin, were American citizens, or had declared their intention to become so, many even of Canadian birth and education having done so, for the advantage it gave them in the region, no alien being allowed to stake and record claims in the American territory of Alaska, while Canada allowed any one to stake and secure title. I informed him that about sixty thousand dollars' worth of goods, local value, entered the territory from American ports every season, but that to attempt to collect customs on them would likely endanger prospecting in our country. Generally, my advice was that, as the country was in a very unsettled state, and our mining laws, so far as known, unsatisfactory to the miners, even of our own nationality, any attempt to take charge of affairs on our side of the line would hinder prospecting by driving most of the prospectors to the American side, and they would stay there till something very rich was discovered in Canada, and that the chance of this would be put back by our action, if we entered with authority then. He agreed with me in this view, as did Mr. Dewdney, the Minister, and I was asked to prepare a memorandum setting forth my views, and the reasons for them, which I did. It was decided to allow things to stand as they were for awhile, but I was directed to keep my eye on the region, and whenever I thought it time to take possession to notify the Department. In September, 1893, I wrote to Mr. Burgess from Juneau, Alaska, where I was in connection with the work of the International Boundary Commission, that I thought it time we were moving in the matter of establishing authority over the Yukon in the goldfields, or we might, if the work were delayed, have to face annoyances, if not complications, through possession, without protest from us, by American citizens. The following summer a North-West Mounted Police officer, Capt. Constantine, and Sergeant Brown from the force were sent in, and formally took possession of Fortymile, by visiting the stores there and requesting and receiving payment of customs due on the goods in them. Some other matters were attended to, and the party continued down the river and returned by the British warship *Pheasant*, then doing duty in Bering Sea. While at Juneau, on his way up, the people of that town strongly impressed Capt. Constantine that nature's route to the Yukon was by Taku Inlet, from the head of which a wagon road could quickly and cheaply be constructed to the head of Lake Teslin, and from there all necessary to be done was to build boats or rafts and float down to any point on the Yukon. He sent a report to his Department urging that the route be examined and adopted. When I returned from my work on the Boundary Commission for the season, I was handed a copy of that part of the report referring to the proposed new wagon route, and asked to report on it. My reply was to the effect that I had met several men who had entered the Yukon valley by this route, and had got from them detailed statements of what they found along it, and the time it took them to cover the distance; that I had also met some who had made their way out over the same route, and had secured from them complete reports, so far as they were competent to give them, of the route. In no case was anything represented to me in the same light as the people of Juneau put it to Capt. Constantine. Further, I had spent much time in Juneau while on the Boundary Commission work in 1893-4, and knew that the people of that town were most anxious to have Juneau become the entrepôt to the Yukon, and as there appeared to be no good harbour or docking-places at the head of Taku Inlet, it was hoped that Juneau would become the terminal port for the route if established. I knew that they had tried to impress me in the same way they did Capt. Constantine, and were most anxious to represent their views as strongly as possible to all whom they thought could bring them before the proper authorities with any hope of notice. Notwithstanding my representations, it was deemed necessary to make an examination of the route, Capt. Constantine's evidence seemed so strong. I protested personally against such a course, as it would involve a great deal to establish what was already as well known as reliable evidence could make it. I was directed to put my Boundary Commission work as quickly as possible into such form that it could be carried on in my absence, and after being at head-quarters only a few weeks, left Ottawa the night of November 30th, 1894, for Juneau. I had arranged for a party of good reliable men to meet me at Victoria, B.C., from where we sailed on the steamer *Mexico* for Juneau. My arrival and mission created quite a sensation. Now it was hoped Juneau would come to her own. Had good wishes availed anything I certainly would have found not only a wagon road, but a railroad, or any other thing that was necessary to fix travel that way to the Yukon now and for ever. A few days were spent securing the necessary outfit, and two boats fit to carry it and the party to the head of Taku Inlet, about twenty-five miles. We got away about noon of December 24th, but owing to heavy loads and contrary wind and tides it was

MR. OGILVIE'S VISIT TO THE COUNTRY

dark, and a very dark night it was too, before we reached Bishop's Point, which forms the lower limit of Taku Inlet. I shall never forget the difficulty of landing here in the pitchy darkness, tramping over slimy rocks, the tide being at its lowest, and just as a blinding snow-storm was coming on, a snow-storm such as is known only by the residents of that region. We unwittingly chose a spot near an Indian encampment, and we were not long there before the dogs of the camp made their presence known. Being acquainted with their thieving propensities, and unable to raise our large tent for the fierce wind, we had to pile our stores in as smooth a heap as we could, and after a hurried supper, laid our beds on the pile to keep the dogs from stealing all we had. As it was, they jerked a pair of boots from under the head of one of the men, who had made a pillow of them, and we never saw the boots after. Three days the storm raged as only storms can rage in these mountain valleys, and we lay waiting for it to subside. The fourth day we rowed hard all day to reach the head of the inlet, only to find more than a mile of it filled with ice from Taku Glacier, which had been held there by the fierce south wind so long that it was frozen together. It began to snow when we landed in a rocky gulch, so we made the best camp we could for the night. Next day I looked over the ice-field for a passage across it, the bank being precipitous and practically impossible ; the only way I could see was to take the small boat, put it on the ice, and walk beside it, hauling it along with us as we went. With two or three hundred pounds in the boat, I took four men, rowed out to the ice and at a safe place pulled out and started hauling the boat over the rough surface, seeking carefully the best places. Occasionally a foot would go through, but the boat was our life-preserver. After a most trying time we reached the head of the inlet, the return was safely made, which, with the gale in our favour, was not so difficult, but we all felt that one such experience was sufficient if a repetition could be avoided, but how to do so was difficult to see. As I lay awake thinking the difficulty over and over, and listening to the rushing of the fierce gale blowing down the inlet, I was startled by one of the most thunderous noises I have ever heard. I had camped in the vicinity of Taku Glacier for some time in the summer of 1893, and knew the tumult it made whenever it shoved, and I knew the noise came from a shove. What the effect was we could not see till morning, when the whole of the head of the inlet was found clear. The glacier had started the two or three square miles of ice, and the gale coming down the river valley had driven it seaward into Stephens Passage, to become the dread of seafarers in the night.

In the teeth of the gale the stores were pulled over to land at the mouth of the Taku River, up which our course lay. Dogs we had none, and if we had they would have eaten more than they could haul. We had to be our own transport motors, and as we had several times more than we could haul at one trip, we had to double and triple trip the way to advance our supplies and outfit. The most gruelling labour got us to the summit of the interior plateau, a micrometer survey of the line of march being made as we went. The most rigid search revealed no practicable wagon road, nothing more than what had been explained to me by the miners I saw who had gone over the route. Two of these, I may mention, were the Day brothers, French-Canadians, to whose reports great respect was paid wherever they were known, and that was pretty widely in the Yukon region.

The return march was begun with bright promise of fine weather, but alas! the second night out the snow began to fall on us as it does in that region near the coast, in great blobs rather than flakes. Of our track up there was no trace, and we sank more than knee-deep in the freshly fallen snow in spite of the large Canadian snowshoes which I had taken, the native kind being too fragile for such long-sustained heavy effort as we had to put forth. The end of our land journey was reached February 24th, and our boat dug out of the five feet of snow that had fallen on it in our absence. Our provisions were exhausted, but we broke into a cache of dried salmon we found at the mouth of the river and took a few of them. After rounding Bishop's Point we were again stopped by one of the fierce winter gales so common in that region, and for three nights and two days we lay shivering and starving at the same time in such shelter as an old cabin could afford. Early in the morning of March 1st we were able to continue our journey to Juneau, which we reached before many of the residents were up. I left the town in December weighing one hundred and ninety-six pounds, and returned tanned by the sun and wind to a bronze hue, and reduced in weight to one hundred and seventy-two. Not many of my friends there recognized me at first sight. Here I learned the heartbreaking news that my dear second son had departed from this world on January 20th. When I left home I knew he was sick, but had hopes of his recovery, and looked with confidence to seeing him again. The shock was a cruel one to me.

When I reached Ottawa I had to prepare a minute report on my expedition and what I saw. Then I had to discuss with Mr. Burgess a scheme he had on foot for the partial organization of the Yukon Territory. This scheme was to appoint an Agent-General, a sort of everything in one, to represent the Government in the territory and administer the laws, and carry out the Government directions. It was proposed to send in

COL. S. B. STEELE, CHIEF FACTOR FOR LAW AND ORDER IN THE YUKON

an adequate number of North-West Mounted Policemen to enforce order and punish lawbreakers, and a sufficient number of assistants, to carry on the work, such as it might prove to be, effectively. The number of policemen was fixed at not less than ten, nor more than twenty. He asked me, if I were taking the office, how many I would consider sufficient, and I replied that I thought ten good reliable men would suffice, as they, I felt sure, would be supported by the good, practical common sense of the community as I knew it. He then told me that I had been selected for the place, and that my salary and allowances would be sufficient to make the position attractive. I asked if I had any choice in the matter, and his reply was that, in view of the bitter experiences I had had during the past winter months, and the sorrow of my loss, if it were very disagreeable to me they would not insist on my accepting, but that it would be very satisfactory if I would. I told him my heart's deepest feelings opposed it, that I did not want to shut myself out from the world, and away from my two remaining boys, who had been brought closer to me by sorrow, and who were now at a critical age, both in education and development, an age that required, I thought, my attention and assistance more than ever. Were the position one that would last only a few months it would be different. He asked me to think it over and try and see my way to accepting. I could not accept, and the scheme was changed somewhat. In a month or so after this Capt. Constantine came to Ottawa, he having been appointed Agent for the territory. He was directed to talk the position over with me and decide how many policemen were necessary. He wanted a much larger number than I thought were required, and we took some time to come to terms on this point. I insisted that twenty were enough, and supported my argument by the fact that there was never any trouble in the country, that my boundary line had been accepted when it might legitimately have been rejected till ratified by the United States, that he had himself gone, alone it might be said, into the territory and collected customs dues without any show of authority. The number was fixed by Mr. Burgess at twenty officers and men, all told. They were to enter the country by the sea route, that is, to St. Michael and up the river. It had been decided before this that I was to visit the country again for a season, and extend the International Boundary Line as far south and north of the Yukon as I thought was necessary, and do any other work that I deemed proper. I did not wish to go, but Mr. Daly, the then Minister, insisted so kindly and considerately, that I could not well refuse.

I decided to go again by the Dyea route, and

chose from my old hands on the Boundary Commission work a good lot of men, and also took my eldest son with me. At the pass I found my old friend Skookum Jim, and his cousin Tagish Charlie, who packed from Sheep Camp to Lake Lyndeman for me. The manager for the firm of Healy and Wilson had organized a horse-packing service from the landing to Sheep Camp, the rest of the way was too steep and rough for horses. On the way down the river I repeated many of the observations I had taken in 1887, especially magnetic ones. Proceeding leisurely we reached Fortymile the last day of August. Here I remained in conference with Capt. Constantine for some days, at the same time adjusting my instruments, repeating observations, and gathering information about some matters of which I had acquired indefinite knowledge in 1887–8. On my way down to the boundary I examined some coal exposures and reported on them to the Agent, in view of applications being made for them, which seemed probable. At the boundary I found our old quarters pretty well wrecked. My observatory had been burned, and a new one had to be erected. When all our preparations for the winter were completed, I arranged for a hunt to secure some fresh meat for the winter months. It may interest many to learn that, just as we were preparing to cross the river on the way to the place I decided to go, one of the men called attention to some dogs, as he thought, walking on the bank on the other side of the river about a mile below us, but a look with the glass resolved, as the astronomer would say, the nebulous mass of dogs into a dense crowd of caribou. As quickly as possible we crossed in our canoe, and in less than a minute after landing had killed six, and in less than half an hour had secured twelve. The females were small compared with the males, and after estimation I decided that it would take at least fifteen to make enough meat to last us the winter, so after dinner I told the men that, if any of them who had not been in the shooting wanted the experience of killing a caribou in the far north, they could go out, shoot one, and then we would put up our guns for the winter. Three elected to do so, went out, and each secured one. Two floated beyond our reach before we could get them ashore, and I killed three more, making in all eighteen killed and sixteen saved. They were almost as tame as cattle. Most of those killed were swimming in the river at the time. They are magnificent swimmers, and could breast current against which two men in one of our light canoes, empty, could not make headway. They were migrating southwards at the time, and remained in thousands around our camp for more than a week. Our houses were objects of great curiosity to them, and numbers of them would swim over, approach the buildings cautiously, whistling and snorting as they did so. They often came so close and were so noisy that they became a nuisance, and we would go out and chase them away. At any time one looked out they were to be seen swimming across the river, and as they were crossing for about ten days, tens of thousands of them must have passed this place. They are migratory, travelling in vast herds, in numbers uncountable. In fall they travel south, and in spring north. The range they travel over is wide, and when they happen to strike near an Indian encampment, there is plenty and contentment there for man and dog, but when, as is often the case, they are scores of miles away, there is starvation and misery for all.

The rifle I used was the ·303 calibre carbine of the British military service, with a twenty-inch barrel. We had other makes in camp of larger calibre, but I never handled a more satisfactory weapon than it proved. But seldom had I to take the second shot at anything when I fired with it. I used altogether the hardnosed bullet, finding it gave the most satisfactory all-round results. It is, indeed, a very convenient weapon for mountain service, short, light, strong, and not easily injured. The new service rifle, with a twenty-four-inch barrel, should prove nearly as handy, and a better shooter. Both are well protected against accidents peculiar to mountain work.

CHAPTER X

WINTER WORK IN 1895–6

THE observatory finished, I set about getting as many observations as possible of the same character as I got in 1887–8. Before cold weather set in I secured six more, which, when reduced and applied to those obtained in 1887–8, left my previous determination practically where it was. I then set about continuing the boundary line northward from the river. I had no instruments of precision with me outside of the astronomical transit. My ordinary line transit was a small three-inch one designed for mountain work. I had to lay down a series of traverse lines with this from the observatory to the boundary line, nearly three miles, and through this traverse I had to originate my boundary line. Those experienced in this kind of work will understand how difficult it would be to lay down a true course from such a source. All the two months I worked on the boundary line I could not get a sight on a star with my transit, such as it was, so the line was run for more than fifty miles

WINTER WORK IN 1895-6

unchecked. It was transited with the baby instrument from peak to peak, sometimes miles apart. The distance from station to station was determined by rough triangulation, which gave results within a few feet of the truth in a mile. At almost every station the camera was set up, and the horizon photographed completely around, in accordance with the system of photo-topography developed so successfully by Capt. E. Deville, Surveyor-General of Canada. This would give a fairly accurate map of the strip along the boundary line of a width of ten miles each side. In addition to this the position and elevation of some distant peaks were determined, and names given them, in nearly all cases perpetuating the names of pioneers.

The work was stopped on April 12th, and I returned to Fortymile to await a stage of water that would permit reasonable progress up-stream and out. While waiting for this, a survey was made of Cudahy and Fortymile town-sites, and some mining claims and land applications laid out. The Canadian Government had entered into a contract with the well-known west-coast veteran, Capt. William Moore, better known as "Old Bill Moore," to carry three mails into the Yukon during the season of 1896. The United States Government had also made a contract with a party to carry mails into the lower Yukon, via the Dyea Pass. The veteran Captain had been over the pass at least twice before, having accompanied me a part of the way down the Yukon in 1887, and later was a few miles past the summit for the British Columbia Government, so he knew how to climb, and better, had some acquaintance with the Indians. Somehow the American contractor got into trouble with his Indians, and was held up about the foot of Lake Bennet, when the Captain came along with the Canadian mail, and though he had only one man with him, and was in his seventy-third year, he, for a consideration, took the American mail along, agreeing to land it at its destination. The Captain brought news to me that precluded all thought of my going out till fall, if not later. The Canadian Government had entered into negotiations with the United States Government for a joint commission to lay down the International Boundary Line with authority, and finally, from the Pacific to the Arctic. I was to be the Canadian Commissioner, and was directed to await further advice on the matter. I was also informed that assistants would likely soon join me with all the necessary outfit. Soon after this I sent my son home by the steamer *Alice*, via St. Michael. I waited anxiously all summer for further advice regarding the international survey, but none came till the Captain's last trip, and I was then advised that the negotiations with the United States had failed, and I was directed to return with all possible dispatch, but dispatch in that region then meant more than it does now. It meant constant physical effort for twenty-five to thirty-five days, making one's way against the strong current of the Yukon, and over the Dyea Pass to the sea. I notified all the people of the vicinity that I would start for the outside in three days, and carry any mail entrusted to me. On the day appointed for my departure the worst storm of rain, with the most violent wind I ever saw in the country, came on, and lasted for three days, culminating in something unprecedented in that region in September, a heavy fall of snow, which covered the ground to a depth of nearly a foot. On October 3rd the river was running thickly with ice, and my trip out was over till the winter at the earliest. The storm appeared to be local, for on October 11th the ice ran past, and on the 14th the steamer *Arctic* made a passage up to the new camp at Dawson, carrying eighty passengers and many tons of much-needed supplies. Ice began to run again in the last days of the month, and winter set in for good. Few who were in the country at that time will forget the very unseasonable weather of the last days of September.

Early in January, 1897, I went up to Dawson to lay out the town-site and survey several other blocks of land applied for there.

COMPLICATIONS ON BONANZA CREEK THROUGH CONFLICTING STAKING OF CLAIMS

I have already referred to a meeting of miners and others on Lower Bonanza Creek at claim No. 17 below discovery, and now I have to take it up again at greater length. When the Mounted Police entered the country the majority of the people were pleased that at last there was some reliable official body representative of law and order in the country, but some who were accustomed to what they called liberty, that is, the privilege, if we may term it so, of doing as they pleased, and paying when they chose, and especially those accustomed to the regulation by each mining community of its own local matters by miners' meetings, and who had not suffered by that system, were opposed to what they styled the interference of the police. At this meeting there were twenty-five, but as in every other crowd, a few did the talking and swayed the meeting. There were only a few pronounced opponents of the police; the rest listened and let things go. At the meeting it was resolved that, as the location of claims so far had been done at random, without any connection between the many locations, therefore it was right and proper that a new and connected survey be made; carried. Resolved further that a local recorder be appointed, and as a "sop" to the public a stranger named David McKay, from Nova Scotia, was elected. It was also resolved that the name of the new creek be Bonanza. A rope was procured, and measured fifty feet long, with which to survey the creek from discovery claim down. A few went up from discovery. Now I afterwards saw seventeen out of the twenty-five present, and examined thirteen of these under oath, but I could never learn who measured the rope, nor to whom it belonged, apparently no one saw it measured. Very good prospects were found on discovery, and just as good on a claim which proved to be sixteen below; what number it was then they could not know, but as it was supposed to be two miles below discovery, and the ground between them was assumed to be all as good, the more claims in the stretch the more people would be enriched. It was agreed between them that the allotment of claims staked that day would be governed by drawing numbers out of a hat. In what way the rope was measured, or how it was held, I do not know, but I do know that discovery claim was cut from four hundred and ninety-six feet, as measured by Carmac, to four hundred and fifty and a half; and No. 1 below from four hundred and ninety-two by Carmac, to four hundred and forty-seven.

Now there was no proper reason why those adjusters could not have been as correct as Carmac, they *had* a measure, he *had none* and trusted to pacing to get the five hundred feet allowed him in each claim. The so-called survey was carried down the creek valley, more than fifty claims in an afternoon; true, the afternoons were long then, from noon till midnight, and claims ranged from three hundred and fifty to four hundred and fifty in the located parts, and more outside of them. They found no room for a claim staked by a previous locator in the vicinity of No. 12 below, so struck him out there and moved him down to fifty below discovery. Only four miles! not much of a move! This man, immediately after locating, had sold his title to the claim to a syndicate of four. One of the first to locate after Carmac was an old man, Edward Monahan, who, on August 19th, located about twenty-nine below, and as he was very friendly with the police officers' wives, and Mrs. Healy, and another lady at Fortymile, after staking his own claim he thought it would be a compliment to the ladies to stake a claim for them too, which he did, and came down and had them recorded through a misunderstanding of the mining regulations.

The adjusters, though they were not opposed to locating absentee men, as there is good reason to suspect was done, and moving one man, as we have seen, from his own location and placing him on another four miles away, were opposed to absentee women being recognized, contrary to the spirit of chivalry we see so often attributed to the miner in stories; so they promptly jumped the claims staked by Monahan for the ladies, and as a warning to all future transgressors like him, jumped his own location also. They then sent a deputation to the Agent, and by misrepresentation to him, as he alleged, induced him to give his official sanction and approval to their acts. Monahan was induced to divide his claim with the jumper, and so the matter ended for awhile, but when the season permitted prospect work to be done, that is, when the frosts tied up all the surface water, and good pay was found, it became an acute question whether or not the new survey would stand. By it many claims were divided between the original locator and the ward of the adjusters, and it was impossible to do full and proper work till the question of ownership was decided. I remember one case where a jumper was put on a claim in such a way that all the original locator had was a few feet of his claim at one end. He was working on this, but was very much cramped in his efforts. In the case of the claim from which the locator was moved to fifty below, neither the purchasers of the original owner's claim, nor the jumper installed by the adjusters, would do anything till the question of legality of location was settled. It seemed impossible to get action on the matter, and as I was not Agent I could not interfere, unless requested by the owners of the claims to make a survey of them, but I had no more authority to step in unasked than I would have to make a survey of a man's town lot, or a farmer's farm, without his request.

I was at last waited on by a deputation, who wanted to learn if it were possible to have something done to settle the muddle things were in. I told them to get up a petition to me to make a survey of all the claims in dispute, or as many of them as possible, and I drafted a form of petition for them, which was copied out on the yellow leaves of a sort of account-book kept by Joe Ladue, the only paper available at the time, and two copies were circulated. In a few days they were returned to me, one containing over fifty signatures and the other over eighty. I walked over the ground where most of the confliction was, and found that, even if there were no more different interests than those caused by abutting claims, there would be trouble, for no one miner or prospector in a hundred ever thinks of the proper manner of staking a claim. At that time the method was intricate, but the motive in framing it was perfectly proper; it was to have each locator so mark his claim, and so surround it by lines, that another locator could not possibly mark one conflicting with it, unless he were physically or, worse, morally blind.

WINTER WORK IN 1895-6

The locator was supposed to plant a post at each corner of his ground, and to cut lines through the woods between them so wide and clear that each post could be seen from the preceding one, unless a hill intervened, in which case the line would lead one to the next post anyway. The locator was supposed to stand facing the south, and post No. 1 would then be over his left shoulder, or at sunrise post No. 2 would be southerly from that up or down the valley, as the case might be, and five hundred feet from No. 1; No. 3 would be across the valley from No. 2, and No. 4 would be up or down the valley from No. 3 and five hundred feet from it. All four posts were to be made not less than three feet in height from the surface of the ground, and not less than three inches square at the top, squared for at least a foot. On No. 1 was to be written legibly, by durable pencil, or inscribed on the post if preferred, the number or other designation of the claim, the name of the locator in full, Christian and surname, the date of location, and the letters M.L.P. and the number of the post as in the order set forth. The above letters stood for Mining Location Post. On the other posts the letters and number of the post only were required, as one finding any of them would know which way to go to find the next in order. I tried very often to get prospectors and miners to see the reasonableness of this method of marking, more especially pointing out that it practically insured them against jumping, for if their lines were so cut out, and posts so marked, very few would care to run foul of the boundaries, and if they did, the presumption of crookedness on their part would be so strong as to amount to absolute proof, but I could never evoke any interest in the method; as one old-timer said to me, "What the h—l's the use of staking at all if you have to represent your claim before recording it?"

In spite of the risk that a claim not legally marked might be lost if another party took the pains to mark the same ground regularly, they were marked in whatever way was most convenient at the time. To mark a claim according to the regulations, as has been outlined, would take a fair axeman about half a day, and when it was done, the locator knew exactly where all his boundaries were, unless he measured more than five hundred feet in length, in which case there would be a fractional claim of the overplus cut off the last end of his claim, that is, a strip the width of the overplus running along the line from post No. 2 to No. 3. As a rule the procedure was to select a tree, knock a bit of bark off it, and proceed to write or scratch on it something like this, "I claim five hundred feet up-stream (or down-stream as the case was) for mining purposes," then date and name, generally only initial for Christian name, or names. Now, if it were

SLUICING ON BANANZA CREEK NO. 2 BELOW

summer-time, and the tree selected was a spruce, which was generally the case, the surface would not only be rough, but very slimy from the sap juices under the bark, and the writing, at best scrawly and poor, would hardly be decipherable. In a few days the flow of gum natural to the spruce would cover the whole face of the cut, and the record, whatever it was, became invisible except to one accustomed to translating such hieroglyphics with the aid of a good magnifying glass. If a poplar were selected, the sap in the tree turned black in a few days after exposure, and the record generally fared as badly as if made on a spruce. If the sap-wood were cut through and a fair surface made, the record was good for an indefinite period. I have often seen records made partly on the sap-wood and partly on the drier wood under it, on which the dry wood retained the record and the sap-wood was completely illegible.

Now, all the difference in time required between making a post that would retain the record for years and one that would retain it for as many weeks, is only a few minutes. A good retentive surface can be prepared by any one so minded in five minutes, but it was not considered necessary to do more than put down something as quickly as possible, which the writer knew the meaning of at the time, but which would take the closest study by others, and most of whom would fail to make anything out of it. Often even the writer, if we may dignify him by such an appellation, could not an hour after, without the aid of his memory, say exactly what he had written. The post or tree marked, the locator then traced a course up or down the valley of the gulch, seeking the easiest places through the brush until he reached the other end of the claim. Here he marked another tree, or made a post, and spent just as little time doing it as possible. One would think it a primary object to be sure that the full five hundred feet was included between the stakes marked, yet in the majority of cases this was not done, which was entirely owing to the course the locator steered while measuring. He made his paces long enough, and counted enough of them, but his base line of measurement was so crooked, or so far away from the middle line of the valley, and so out of parallel with it, that the claim was short in measure. The mathematical principles underlying this are so simple that one would think them perfectly obvious, and that a little torment from mosquitoes, or a biting cold, could not drive them from their minds, but so it appeared. From the upper end of discovery claim to the lower end of sixty below, as laid out, there are sixty-one claims, yet the measurement shows it sufficient for fifty-two full claims only. I remember one instance where the locator so meandered that his lower stake

WINTER WORK IN 1895-6

was actually twelve feet farther up the valley than his upper one, that is, he had actually staked twelve feet less than nothing, and as he had sold the claim (No. 12 below mentioned) the location had to be considered, and by adjusting the boundaries above it I succeeded in allotting it three hundred and eighteen feet, without interfering with any rights. In another case a locator had so meandered in his pacing that I could not possibly give him more than one hundred and thirty-eight feet between his stakes.

The reader will see from this, that with the confusion of two different sets of stakes planted, and the resultant confliction of development work, there was no easy task before me in trying to do justice. First I saw as many of the parties present at the meeting of August 22nd as I could conveniently reach, and under the provisions of the Survey Act examined them as fully as possible regarding the motives and acts of those present. Most of those I saw now perceived the folly of their attitude at the meeting, and the mischief that had resulted therefrom, and were heartily with me in my endeavour to adjust matters, and assured me that whatever I did would be satisfactory if the muddle were only settled. A few, however, of the members stuck to their original ideas, and held that, as the Agent had assented to what they had done and put it on record, it was good and valid. I could not accept this view, and proceeded to wipe out their work wherever it conflicted with any previous location. There was no active objection to my doing so, but there was some " wild and woolly " talk. One or two who hailed from freeman's land seemed to think that something was required of them, and accordingly, if report be true, talked of shooting, and other violent measures, if their locations were interfered with. A few of my friends took a serious view of this and warned me to be careful, but it did not seem to me that the threats amounted to more than letting off a cloud of steam to back out of, unseen. As the work proceeded this kind of talk quietened down, and when I came to the location of the man who, according to report, did most of the threatening, even to saying he would shoot me if I came on his claim, my base line ran into his cabin, and I had to set my transit on the roof to carry the line over. This I did in peace, and without objection, though the occupant was in the cabin at the time. When I descended he came out, and laughingly asked me what I was doing. I told him, and was then invited in to dinner, which I accepted. During the meal he inquired if I were going to put him off the claim he was on, and to my great surprise, when I told him I was, he accepted the dictum very gracefully, and asked me what I would advise him to do in the future ; go and look up new ground and get a full claim,

WINTER WORK IN 1895-6

or accept a fraction of a hundred feet that was still open ? I was a good deal surprised by this sudden change of front, for I could not doubt all my informants about this man's attitude, and was very cautious about advising him in any direction till his sincerity appeared real to me. After some discussion as to his means and position, I advised him to take the fraction as the best thing he could do at that time. He thanked me, and we parted good friends, he going that afternoon to locate the fraction in question, and so the noise ended.

The noise ended, but four or five of the quieter protestants held a meeting and appointed a deputation of three to wait on and learn from me if they could not do something in the way of presenting their case to Ottawa that would secure them some consideration, for, as they said, they hated to be left out in the cold entirely. This was even a greater surprise to me than the surrender of the belligerent individual just mentioned. The conference was held in a vacant cabin, so was on neutral ground. I asked the deputation to state its case as concisely as possible. It was simply a recital of what I had heard very often before, to wit, they had been sincere in their attitude at the meeting, and had acted aboveboard and in good faith, having an eye single to the best interests of the community in all they did. Now it was quite evident to me, from remarks that were dropped from time to time by those I had examined as to the doings and sayings at the meeting, that the meeting was, on the part of the ringleaders at least, a protest against interference with their rights. They considered, as they had been left so long to the direction of their own affairs, that the intrusion of authority and policemen to uphold it was an usurpation. As I have said before, only a few held this view, but that few insinuatingly tried to present it and have it acknowledged as widely as possible. Knowing this, I was not much impressed by the protestations of good faith, though I did not say anything. I told them if they wished to present their case to Ottawa, that was their privilege, and I would give them any assistance I could in so doing. They asked me if I would endorse their position, which I emphatically assured them I would not, but on the contrary would report against it as strongly as I could. After some discussion as to how the matter of their petition should be arranged, I rose to go, remarking as I did so, " Whenever you are ready, gentlemen, call on me, and I will be glad to assist you in getting up your petition, but just before I go I want to say to you that the most peculiar feature of the case, as it presents itself to me, is the position you are in yourselves."

I was asked what I meant, and replied, " In the application you made when applying for the claims you recorded, you swore that, ' to the best of your knowledge and belief, the land you applied for was vacant Dominion land, and that in staking you had not encroached on any occupied ground.' Now there is a provision in the Criminal Code of Canada that 'any one who knowingly and wilfully removes, defaces, alters, or destroys any post or monument planted, placed, or marked as a boundary or limit of any parcel or tract of land whatsoever may be imprisoned in the penetentiary for five years.' Now if you can convince the officers of the Department of the Interior, or a disinterested jury, that you collectively went down this creek in the afternoon of August 22nd last, removing, defacing, altering, and destroying every post you could find that interfered with your programme, and putting yourselves on the claims so located ; and that you did not see those posts while you were doing this, why, you may stand clear in your record. But if they do not believe you, you are liable to criminal prosecution of a serious nature. Another thing I must say is, that your claim to recognition, because you were officially recognized, will not afford you that support you seem to think so strong, for the Agent will declare that he recognized you through misrepresentation on your part, and his affirmation under the circumstances will be at least of as much force as yours. Good night, gentlemen ; when you want me, call on me."

As I was picking up my snow-shoes outside, I overheard the spokesman for the party remark " It's a —— —— fizzle," and laugh. I heard no more about a reference to Ottawa. Nor was the trouble ever again referred to as a right by any one. I have spoken of this matter at some length, because it was a thing of much interest and excitement at the time, and as an instance of what may occur in mining camps, not on as large a scale, perhaps, but many times posts are either not seen, and the ground re-located, or, worse still, the posts destroyed, or the record on them removed and another put on, and then it is a case of who can swear most. Our Territorial Judges could tell something about this subject. At the time I speak of, the method of marking out a claim was intricate, no doubt, as I have described, but it was worth all the trouble and more to the locator if he would only follow it out, for it put him on record on the ground in a very patent way, but the method was not generally known, for only the Agent and myself had copies of the regulations, and so but few saw them. Now, however, each paper in the Yukon Territory publishes in every issue a résumé of the mining regulations sufficient to acquaint any one with all that is necessary to properly locate, mark, and record a claim. Yet I will venture the assertion that not more than twenty-five per cent of the claims are marked any way near the legal manner. It is now illegal to mark a tree as a post bounding a claim; a tree may be used, but it must be cut off at the legal height, and flatted or squared so as to present the appearance of a post. A line must be marked or opened out in the woods, between the posts, to make it evident to prospectors that some one else has been there before. As an illustration of how it is really done, I may describe what I found in 1908, when looking for the boundaries of nine claims I wanted to examine. The party of nine was led by two commissioners for taking affidavits, one of whom is called a mining engineer. To these we should look for something approaching precision, yet I found that all the posts but one were trees, only one of which had been cut off to make it a post, which was not, however, either the legal height or size. Only one record was readily decipherable, four of them undecipherable, and all the rest were more or less so, yet they had been marked less than three months.

Immediately after the staking, one of the commissioners took the affidavits of the men that they had " marked out on the ground, in accordance in every particular with the Dominion Mining Regulations, the claim hereby applied for "; knowing, if he knew anything, that they did not. The measurement was made in such a careless way that the whole bunch of claims did not cover more than two-thirds of the ground mentioned. In the case of the one staked by the mining engineer, it will not, when surveyed, be more than one hundred and fifty feet long, instead of five hundred, as allowed by the regulations. I dwell on this feature because it seems so remarkable to me, and I am sure would to the public too, if it could only see it, and realize the result of such criminal ignorance and neglect in the disputes and lawsuits for which it is responsible. There is no excuse for it now. There might have been some in the early years. I do not mean that all claims are shorter than they ought to be; many locators are shrewd enough to be sure to take enough, knowing that all they have over five hundred feet will be separated as a fractional claim whenever a survey is made. I know one case where nine hundred and forty-two feet were paced off, and the justification was that it was done in the dark, and the party could not see to count his steps. The real motive was to secure a claim for an absent friend, but " the best laid schemes o' mice and men," etc.; before the friend came another man discovered the extra length, located it, and is now a wealthy resident of a western city.

CHAPTER XI

WORK DONE ON THE CREEKS BY MR. OGILVIE

I SURVEYED one hundred and twenty claims on Bonanza Creek, and fifty on Eldorado Creek, and by that time, April 12th, the snow was melting so fast, and the water so deep in places, that further work could not well be done. During the progress of the work I lived with the miners, and they furnished the help necessary on the work. My time was paid for by the Government, so the survey cost the claim-holders but little. I can never forget the universal kindness and consideration of the people as a whole, in the midst of a great excitement; for there are few other conditions as exciting as the inception of a great mining camp. I once heard a prominent Englishman, in an address he was making in London, declare that there were two great calamities that could befall a country, and he could not say which was the worst : " War, or the discovery of gold." This may be an exaggeration, but, certainly, when the microbe of gold-fever, fresh from the shafts, drifts, and sluice-boxes of the field, gets into the blood, the temperature rises till delirium sets in and even the best of men are hardly themselves. Think of it, reader; a man may apparently have been doomed to a lifetime of toil, of pinching here and pulling there to make ends meet, hoping and longing for what he must feel he can never have; what it means to be suddenly thrust into a field where he may any hour, unknown to himself, mark out millions for the digging. Is it any wonder that men, and women too, lose their heads and become for the time what they never dreamed of becoming? Is it any wonder that a gold-mad camp has been compared to war, and war has been compared to some place far south of Klondike!

Sitting with the miners in the long evenings, much talk was indulged in about many things, and the mining regulations came in for a large share of comment and criticism, and truly they were at that time not quite suited to the needs of such a bleak clime. Many suggestions were made and discussed as to amendments. These were all carefully noted and sent to Ottawa at the first opportunity, from which followed many changes. The old method of marking out a claim was simplified to practically the present method, which, as we have seen, is not observed much, if any, better than the old way. The age of a locator was lowered from twenty-one to eighteen, the objectionable formula in the affidavit of application, "I solemnly swear that

I have discovered therein a deposit of gold," which very few ever did, for the simple reason they did not look for it, was changed to " I solemnly swear that I have reason to believe there is therein a deposit of gold." It is astonishing to reflect that thousands of claims were staked and recorded in the Klondike particularly, and Yukon generally, and in few was any attempt made at all to find gold. Some one had found gold somewhere on the creek or bench. That was enough ; every one who recorded did so on the strength of that find. The spirit of the law in those days was that each individual should thoroughly prospect his claim before applying for record, and he was given sixty days in which to do it. I attribute much of the apparently criminal conduct to the slipshod way affidavits are generally read over ; in fact, they are very often not read at all ; it seems to be the desire to get through with the job as soon as possible.

While making the survey, one of my duties was to take the affidavits of application of locators who did not wish to make the journey to Fortymile, sixty odd miles, to the Agent's office, the only place they could record at the time. The regulations permitted a locator to make the affidavit of application before any Justice of the Peace or Commissioner, and as I had been made a Commissioner of Police before my first entry to the country I was qualified to serve the miners in that way. The affidavit, with the necessary fee for record, was sent to the Agent's office by the first opportunity, and the record was counted from the date the affidavit was sworn to. In every case before swearing the attestor I read it over slowly and carefully, and in many cases the proceedings stopped there, for the applicant had not discovered gold, had not looked for it, and, of course, he could not swear to something he had not done. In many instances, however, I felt sure the oath was taken in spite of the fact that no search had been made for the precious metal. I remember one instance where a man came to me to have his affidavit taken who bore the reputation of being the toughest citizen of Dawson at that time, before the rush, and I did not look for any conscientious scruples on his part. When his affidavit was completed I read it over to him; as soon as the words " I have discovered therein a deposit of gold " were spoken, he stopped me sharply with the exclamation, " But I have not ! I did not look for any." " Then you cannot take this oath," I said.

After explanation, it turned out he did not know the requirements, thinking it only necessary to stake the ground. He had only forty-eight hours in which to return to the claim, prospect it, find gold, and complete recording by making the affidavit. If he failed he might lose it altogether, for another party, knowing it was not recorded, had staked it, anticipating failure to record within the legal time. He started immediately for the claim, it being highly desirable to avoid, if possible, any question of loss of title through its having been re-staked before the sixty days expired. He reached the ground the next evening after travelling all night, fed and tied up his dogs, gathered dry wood, built a fire, thawed the ice off the gravel, and built another fire to thaw the gravel itself, washed all he had thawed, and did not find a colour! He selected another place, thawed again, washed and found three small colours, but unmistakably gold, started back, and reached Dawson about eleven at night, showed me the gold, made his oath, and saved his title by an hour, after being on the jump for forty-eight hours without rest, and with very little nourishment. When all was completed he remarked, "Mr. Ogilvie, I am considered a hard case here, and there are more want to pass me than speak to me, yet I would not have taken that oath to save my claim, not for all the claims in the Klondike," and I believed him. It is poor, poor ground where there is not some pay streak.

Contrast this with another case about the same time. When I read over the affidavit, and the formula above-cited was spoken, he was startled into the exclamation, "But, by golly, I didn't find any, I didn't look for it."

"Well," I said, "you cannot take this oath."

He went away, and the claim was recorded somehow. A few were so scrupulous that when they discovered they had unwittingly sworn to an untruth, they went to the trouble of re-locating their claims, and recorded them a second time, having, of course, to pay a second fee.

As I have said, every consideration was extended me while on the creeks. It seemed I was considered a sort of arbiter in all disputes, and as my knowledge of law was very limited, no question of jurisdiction was ever raised, nor was any decision I ever made objected to in any active way. I had to decide against some one in every dispute, yet I never noticed any feeling of animosity on account of it, and I think that speaks well for the law-abiding sentiments of the people then in the country. There were no policemen nearer than sixty-five miles, and even had there been they were so few in number that, if lawlessness predominated, they could not have done very much to restrain it.

The reader will have gathered that, while making the survey of the claims, many questions arose that in older communities would have involved lawsuits; my position was in consequence sometimes a trying one. In many cases I had to fling law and the principles of boundary adjustment aside, and make such adjustment of limits as would save to innocent people the result of months of trying labour. I recall one case in

WORK DONE ON THE CREEKS

particular, when a rigid adherence to the law governing surveys would have cut a poor miner out of the result of nearly five months' labour, and compelled him to begin over again too late in the season to accomplish more than pay the great expense he had incurred under the very exceptional conditions of the winter and even that satisfaction might have been doubtful. The parties adjoining this boundary had no idea of the quandary I was in for a time, and the one to whom I extended the favour of the doubt is now a wealthy resident on the Pacific coast. The other one, though he had equally as good ground as his neighbour, lost all, some are unkind enough to say through his own act, and is still resorting to the territory in search of fortune. So the sequel to my decision, in a manner, eased my conscience on the irregularity of the boundary.

The measurements on the survey were made with a Gunter's chain of sixty-six feet in length divided into one hundred links, and as the measurement on my bases was continuous no one but myself knew whether a claim was long or short, or how much so, until I told it. In this way I was enabled to conceal the existence of fractional claims, which I made known only by marking them on the posts bounding the end, not the beginning of the claim. In only one case did I depart from this rule, and that time I felt the circumstances justified it.

Mr. Clarence Berry, of California, was the fortunate owner of a half-interest in claims Nos. 3, 4, 5, and 6, on Eldorado Creek. He and his partner decided to do all their work for the season on the upper end of claim No. 5. Such a thing as there being an overplus of measurement in this claim did not occur to them. Fortunately for them and the community, I reached the limit of claim No. 5 in the evening, just as the men were quitting work in the shafts below, and as it had been a cold, windy day—ten below zero—I, too, thought it time to quit, so directed my men to take my instruments to a near-by cabin. I then turned to my notes to figure out the length of the claim, the men, meanwhile, standing around me guessing what I was doing, and anxious to learn how the claim turned out in size. I never suspected a fraction here; such diligent search having been made for them in all the rich ground that it seemed impossible for one to escape. My calculations showed that claim No. 5 was five hundred and forty-one feet six inches long, thus opening a fractional claim of forty-one feet six inches to location. And such a location! Possibly in all the history of gold-mining none was ever found richer; single pans—two shovels of dirt—were found in it with values as high as five hundred dollars in gold. Fifty, sixty, and so on to one-hundred-and-fifty-dollar pans were quite common.

Nearly all the work so far done—and it was near

DUMP ON CLAIMS 5 AND 6, ELDORADO

WORK DONE ON THE CREEKS

the close of the season—had been done on this fraction. The discovery brought from me, by way of exclamation, a whistle, which I at once recognized would cause suspicion, and maybe investigation. So, to allay it, I turned to the men and repeated to them in more detail my instructions regarding the instruments, then said to Berry, "Let us go to supper, Berry; I am cold enough and hungry enough to eat nuggets," and started on a quick walk to his cabin, a short distance away. The men, however, did not do as I directed them; they seemed to have suspected something, and gathered in a group, and engaged in what appeared to me, as well as I could see by hurried glances over my shoulder, an animated discussion. Berry, also, was alarmed, and as we were walking hurriedly to his cabin, asked me, in too loud a tone I thought, " Is there anything wrong, Mr. Ogilvie ? " I whispered, " Come on out of hearing," but he could hardly wait, and kept asking, " What is wrong ? My God ! what is wrong ? " When we were well out of hearing I said, without slackening my pace, for the men, I could see, were still watching us, " There is a fraction of forty-one feet six inches on claim No. 5, and nearly all your winter's work is on it." " My God ! " he exclaimed in a loud voice, " and all our work on it too; surely it cannot be so; tell me it is not so ! What will I do ? " I replied, " I cannot advise you; it is not my place to do so"; but he insisted on my making some suggestion. Under the pressure of his alarm I said, " Have you not a friend you can trust ? " " Trust, how ? " " Why, to stake that fraction to-night, and transfer it to yourself and partner." At the suggestion the name of the same individual occurred to both of us—George Byrne—and it was decided that Berry should at once go to where he was at work on a claim five miles farther up the creek, and I would await his arrival at Berry's cabin. In the cabin Berry, without much ceremony, told Mrs. Berry to get me my supper at once and not wait for him, as he had to run up the creek a bit to see a man.

She, naturally enough for either man or woman, wanted to know what the rush was about. " Could he not wait for his supper after such a cold, hard day ? " And so on. He, however, bolted in the midst of her inquiries, leaving me to dispel her curiosity as best I could. Between nine and ten o'clock Berry returned with Byrne, and shortly after we all sat down to another hearty supper. During supper, Byrne, who was a well-educated, intelligent man, made minute inquiries regarding the legal method of staking a claim; staking and marking it in such a way that there would be no doubt about the title. Mr. Byrne gave as his reason for the inquiry the fact that he had not yet been fortunate enough to find a bit of ground he

WORK DONE ON THE CREEKS

thought worth taking, which both Berry and I knew, when his name occurred to us, and so he could legally stake the fraction. No one would suspect, either from his language or looks, or mine, that we had more than a general informational interest in the matter. After supper I took a sheet of wrapping paper and made a detailed plan of the method of staking and marking both a full claim and a fractional one, which I gave to him, and was rewarded with a profusion of the most formal thanks. We each, though knowing exactly what was in the mind of the other, concealed it by what I may with true modesty call good acting. Certainly Mrs. Berry did not suspect anything.

In the early hours of the morning, when every one but Berry and Byrne was asleep, Byrne staked the fraction, conforming strictly to the law, and when the workmen arose and saw what had been done, the comment was as loud and coloured as the fraction was rich.

An estimate of the value of the dump—pile of pay dirt taken out—placed it at one hundred and thirty thousand dollars. It cleaned up more then one hundred and thirty-six thousand in the spring.

The reader is invited to imagine what a wild scramble there would have been had all the labourers present tried to stake that rich fraction at the same time, for they all had an idea of its great value. It is not at all unlikely that some one would have been hurt; and the dispute that would have followed as to who was the first to complete staking would have been a hard nut for the Agent, Capt. Constantine, to crack.

Mr. Byrne at once assigned all his interest in the fractional claim to Berry and partner, receiving in consideration an equal length off the lower end of claim No. 3, so that Berry and partner retained an unbroken block. It does not appear, however, that the ground Byrne got was nearly as valuable as the ground he gave. A friend like that, in such a need, is a friend indeed.

As an example of the excitement and spirit the possible acquisition of a rich, or supposedly rich, claim can create, the following occurrences serve well.

The ownership of one of the last claims staked on upper Bonanza Creek lapsed about the end of November, 1896, through the locator having failed to record location within the period fixed by the regulations, and extended by the Agent on account of the difficulty of travelling in the early winter months. As it turned out, the claim was worthless, nothing of value being found past claim No. 42 above discovery on that creek, but this was not known at the time. It was certain that the locator had gone from the country, and at that season of the year there was little likelihood of his returning in time to make record, so some twelve or fourteen decided to re-stake it and record. As it was evident that several would attempt to locate the claim, and all would be on the ground at midnight of the last day, it was deemed wise to send a member of the North-West Mounted Police force, several of which were at Dawson at the time, to see that there was no disturbance, and to announce the hour of midnight officially. When the intending locators met on the ground it became plainly evident that it would be farcical for all to try and stake at the same time and then be positively certain who was the first to finish marking. So all dropped out but two, one a Canadian, named John Van Iderstein, commonly known as Johnny Van. Strange to say, the possessor of this name was nearly pure Scotch in descent, his mother being Highland Scotch of so pronounced a character that she read her Gaelic Bible and offered up her daily supplications in her native tongue. His father was Scotch, it might be said, in everything but name. One day, while conversing with him, I suggested that, in view of his parentage and the misleading character of his name, he ought to set himself right before the public by changing the Van to Mac or Mc and call himself McIderstein, but there was not the necessary authority there to make the change.

The other man was, I think, a Swede, whose

name I cannot now recall. All the others, though out of the contest, in spite of the bitter cold, remained to see the race. The two prepared stakes, on which was fully written the customary record, and both repaired to the starting-point, ready for action when the policeman should call time; that called, both stakes were driven simultaneously, and a race for the other end of the claim, five hundred feet away, began. It ended in a tie as nearly as those present could decide, and then the great race to Fortymile—more than seventy-five miles away—began. Down Bonanza Creek they fled on foot, soon leaving the other intending locators and policeman far behind. Dawson, eighteen miles away, was reached in the early morning hours, and the news of the race for a claim set the town on fire. Each contestant had friends, who determined to aid their choice in every way possible. A hearty breakfast was hurriedly eaten, and dog-teams as hurriedly prepared, both as lightly loaded as practicable, for every superfluous pound lessened the chance of victory; then away they flew on the long sixty-mile home stretch of the race. Each knew that the office at Fortymile closed at four o'clock in the evening, and if they did not reach it before that hour, they would have to wait till nine o'clock the next morning, and after such a long race a night's repose might lessen their zeal through stiffened limbs and strained muscles, so every effort was put forth to reach the goal that evening. How they passed and repassed each other ; how they jockeyed or manœuvred will never be known, for but these two witnessed the race, and they were too busy to pay any attention to details ; the great desideratum of modern business methods— RESULTS—was all they thought of. Within two or three miles of the office the Canadian's dogs began to flag, and no urging, no punishment, could increase their speed. They were, in the slang of the day, " all in." The Swede was coming up, and slowly but surely passing. Jumping ahead of his team, the Canadian left it to finish on foot ; the Swede was not to be so beaten, and he, too, left his team. On they went, neck and neck through the barrack-yard gate, the goal now only a few yards away, and each spent and panting for breath. The Swede was not acquainted with the arrangement of the buildings in the barrack square, and made straight for the largest building he saw—the officers' quarters. The Canadian was familiar with the place and knew the recorder's office was on the right-hand side of the square, and letting the Swede pass, he turned sharply to the right, reached the office door, opened it, but was unable to raise his foot over the threshold—about six inches high—and fell prone on the floor across it, shouting as he did so, " Sixty above on Bonanza," the designation of the claim, which the Swede, momentarily thrown out of the race by his ignorance, echoed as he fell over the Canadian a second later.

When they were sufficiently recovered to talk, the story was told, and the race being a tie from start to finish, the Agent advised them to divide the claim between them, which was done. Before the winter passed the ground was known to be worthless, but the memory of the great race remains with them yet.

Another race worthy of record was made against time by a Finn, and is a good example of the practical jokes common in mining camps, or in any community of men endowed with the abundant animal spirits the pure air and good exercise found in the North bestows on the great majority of its residents. This man, commonly known as Charlie the Finn—I do not know his surname—had located a claim on the branch of Bonanza Creek, entering at well above the pay ground called "Ready Bullion Creek." It appeared that none of the locators on the creek were able, for lack of funds or outfit, to do any developing work, and its value was for many months an unsolved problem. Well along in the winter Charlie went down from the mines to Dawson to try his luck at getting an outfit. Being of a hopeful, boasting nature, he could not help talking about his claim and the great good fortune it was going to yield him. To all willing to listen he would enter into a detailed calculation of how he was going to

NORTHERN DOG TEAM

work, what the result would be, and his happy return to that girl in Finland. In two or three days this became monotonous and the boys determined to stop it, so fixed up a little job. It was known that Charlie had not yet recorded his location, and that only a few days of the probation term remained for him to do it in, and thereby hangs this tale. While Charlie was holding forth eloquently to some, this time eager listeners, two new men came in, " Howdy'd " to the others in the saloon, went to the bar and called for a drink, in which the bar-tender was invited to join. After the drink the bar-tender, who, of course, was in the secret, asked them " where they came from and how things were doin'." The replies in whispers, loud enough, however, for Charlie to hear, were, that " they had just come in from the vicinity of Ready Bullion, where something rich had been struck, something that knocked Bonanza, Eldorado, Hunker, and all the other creeks into a cocked hat." One after another of the listeners joined the group, and soon all were engaged in animated discussion of the new find and its possibilities ; all but Charlie, who, knowing his claim was not recorded, was prudent enough to say nothing more than ask a casual question once in a while. Soon one of the new-comers asked "if any one knew who owned claim number six on the Creek. He had accounted for all the others and tried to get one of them, and his only chance was that claim, which he could not place, as the writing on the location posts was impossible to read; further, he had been told that the locator had never recorded, and if he could learn that positively, he would go right out there, locate and record at once." Poor Charlie could stand no more, and left as quietly as possible, rushed over to his cabin, seized some cold pancakes—all the food left over from his self-cooked breakfast—and without any more clothing than he wore in the house, started on foot for Fortymile to record his claim, having still a few days left in which to do so. The only cabin he could rest in was about eighteen miles down the river. About nine miles down a man with a team of dogs coming up met a solitary individual running as if for his life, streaming with perspiration, carrying his cap in one hand, and some frozen pancakes in the other. Thinking this individual mad or criminal, he tried to stop him, but he was past almost before the dog driver could stop his team, and in answer to inquiries, "Where are you going? What are you running for?" all that could be heard was something about "Number Six, Ready Bullion, struck it rich"; and he was out of hearing. Meanwhile the parties to the joke missed Charlie and made search for him, but the day being cold and windy and but few outdoors, it chanced no one had seen him leave. It was not until the dog driver reached town that the mystery was cleared up,

WORK DONE ON THE CREEKS

and then serious fears were entertained lest the poor half-clad, half-fed man would perish on the long, lonely sixty-mile race. He reached Fortymile next day, recorded his claim, and raised an excitement almost equal to his own about Ready Bullion. Alas for poor Charlie and many others like him! Ready Bullion proved no bullion at all, and as far as I have ever learned, that girl in Finland is still waiting. Some time after, when Charlie had learned of the trick that had been played on him, I met him and innocently remarked, " Well, Charlie, that was a great race you had." What he said in reply has made me regret ever since that I mentioned it.

Practical jokes of this kind were sometimes successfully played by " Chechakos " (new-comers) on " Sour Doughs " (old-timers). An instance of this was the trick played on Joe Ladue in the spring of 1897. Harry Ash, a " Chechako " from Juneau, had brought with him some very fine specimens of gold-bearing quartz. Now, Joe's satisfaction with the results of the past winter's work in the Klondike was almost perfect; the only thing required to round it out to absolute perfection was the discovery of a big vein of gold-bearing rock; but Joe had remarked in a tone of conviction, " She's comin', boys ; she's comin' ! " One of Joe's associates in business thought it would be a pity to disappoint him, and arranged with Ash to put up a job on him. Ash then began to show, in strict confidence, some of his specimens of quartz, with mysterious hints that their source was not very far away. Among the favoured few was, of course, Joe's partner, who, beaming with joy, took him into the secret, with strict injunctions not to mention the matter to a soul, as Ash was not ready for proclamation yet, having first to stake, and so fix his record as to make himself absolutely safe. As evidence of what was communicated, specimens of the gold-bearing quartz were shown. This was more than flesh and blood could stand, at least more than Joe's could stand; he called on Ash, and by many winks and nods let him know that he was "wise" to some things supposed to be profound secrets. Ash, of course, affected great chagrin that his secret was revealed, and "wanted to know who talked." Joe would not tell, but vowed eternal silence if he were let in. Ash told him "he could not yet proclaim the find, as was the custom, but would let him (Joe) in just as soon as he had seen Mr. Ogilvie and learned all about how to locate and record a quartz claim." Joe, being on very good terms with me, undertook to see me and hurry the matter along. Ash and he called on me, and by diagram I fully explained to them the way to locate, mark, and record a quartz claim. I asked no questions, but after the meeting Joe came to me and in the strictest confidence—of course—told me all he knew, and as proof of what he said showed me a small bit of the rock, which certainly looked good.

Ash was to stake that day, and then Joe would be given the tip. He would go out, find the place, then signal me by fires, and I was to go out with my instruments, trace the lode as far as possible beyond Ash's location, when Joe would stake on the continuation, to be followed by myself if I wished, then Joe's partner, and we would all be rich, " Everlastingly rich! Have barrels of money." Soon after Joe left his partner saw me, put me " wise," as he termed it, to the whole plot, and told me that six others with Joe were to be victimized; all the seven being selected on account of their assumed superior knowledge of mining—quartz mining particularly. At the appointed time all seven were separately given the tip, each being led to believe that he was the only one. They started very secretly from seven different points. Arrived at the scene of action, it was not long before each began to see that others were in the woods, and as secrecy had been absolutely required of them, and was necessary to success, for each, like Joe, had friends to follow, they spent the whole day dodging each other. When they returned, tired and hungry, in the evening, the chaffing and greetings accorded them can best be left to the imagination.

That mines would be salted, that is, prepared with gold-dust to tempt inexperienced purchasers, might be thought impossible in such a community of "generally" experienced men; but it was tried on two or three occasions. In one instance the intended victims were well-known miners, natives of the Province of New Brunswick. The promoter of the scheme was a Swede, an alleged retired sea captain, noted for a craftiness in his dealings that rather prejudiced his neighbours against him. During the survey of the claims on the Klondike creeks, this man tried to make use of me for his own advantage, and as he said for mine too, and it took a good deal of blunt talk to convince him that he was on the wrong scent: but to our tale of salting, though his attempts with me might well be called that. He and his partner were working two claims on a branch of the Fortymile River, which were not paying too much. Our crafty ex-captain thought they might "strike it rich" by a more indirect method than mining, and resolved to try it. One morning, soon after the resolve was made, he clothed himself in "sackcloth and ashes," so to speak, and called on our friends from New Brunswick. He was invited to breakfast, but felt much too bad to eat anything. Kindly inquiry after cause of his indisposition was answered, in a voice full of tears, by the information that his partner was seriously ill with a complaint that only a long course of hospital treatment could hopefully deal with, and there being no hospitals nearer than

Victoria, B.C.—there was no Vancouver then—to get him out in time to save his life meant everything, and a good deal more money than they had, unless they could sell their claim. Much sympathy was shown for the sick man and inquiries made by the intended victims to learn if something could not be done to help, or if the community could not assist in some way. But the broken voice assured them nothing but a hospital treatment by a specialist would avail anything; that the sick man had been treated for the same disease once before and warned that a recurrence of it, unless speedily dealt with, might, probably would, be a matter of life and death. The plan of getting him out was gone over, the details settled, and then the question of means came up. A canvass of the camp to raise by subscription the amount required the sorrowing partner would not listen to; it would take too long, too precious time would be lost, and the man might die before starting, or on the way out. The only way that would ensure any chance of successful treatment was to sell their two claims for what they could get for them, and with that and the little they had they could probably get out and defray the hospital expenses. The claims were certainly worth much more than they were forced by misfortune to offer them for, which was five hundred dollars each. A visit to the sick man, and the claims, was arranged for the following morning, and they would see what could be done. The wily one left much comforted by the prospect for his partner's speedy relief and tried to express his gratitude, but his broken voice and tear-brimming eyes did that more eloquently than mere words could do. The following morning the visit was paid, the sick man found in bed, and a very sick man he was if moans and appearances could indicate it. The wily one was so overpowered by his partner's pain that he showed but little attention to the visitors; in a shaking voice he directed them to a shaft in which he had put a fire the night before, and requested them to clean it out, he had not had time to do so, and pan the dirt for themselves. They did so, and the result satisfied them; the claims were worth buying. Returning to the cabin, they arranged to buy the claims for five hundred dollars each, handing over what dust they had brought with them, nearly all the proceeds of the season's work so far, and gave an order on Jack McQuesten for the balance. A transfer of the property was drawn up and signed, by the sick man with great difficulty and much pain.

The victims returned to their cabins, about a mile away, and being near noon one of them began preparing dinner while the other unwrapped the result of their panning in the newly bought claims and put it under a magnifying glass for examination. It did not take him long to see what they

WORK DONE ON THE CREEKS

had found, and he was startled into the exclamation, " Well I'll be ——! " " What is the matter, Skiff ? " was the almost equally vehement inquiry. " H—l, it's amalgam, Jack ! " " No ? " " Yes, come and see ! " He did ; a critical look convinced them that they had been fooled. To put on his coat and cap was the work of an instant, and to snatch his 45-calibre revolver and jump for the track to the new claims, another. Arrived at the cabin, it was found empty, and the "Yukon sleighs," together with all the bedding and outfit they had, were gone. It was, indeed, a case of sudden repair to the hospital. To follow them was the resolution of a moment, and as they had each a heavily laden sleigh, overtaking them was only a matter of time. He came suddenly upon them nearly half-way to Fortymile, and "hands up" was the order of the day. They were ordered to step away from their sleighs, hand over the dust paid them on account and the order on Jack McQuesten for the balance ; this done they were thrown their transfer of the claims, and told to go on as fast as possible. The sick man had, apparently, fully recovered since morning and the pair continued to Fortymile ; the claims not being worth further effort. Jack and Skiff both told me the story and seemed to enjoy the recollection. It is interesting to reflect on what the result of an appeal to a Judicial Court would have been in this case, had there been one there at the time, and the wily one and partner had appealed to it. Would Jack and Skiff, as is very often the case when honest men come into conflict with "crooks," have been unfortunate?

Some may not know what Skiff meant when he exclaimed "It's amalgam, Jack," so I will explain. It is very difficult—sometimes practically impossible—to separate fine gold from the gravel, sand, and black sand associated with it, without the aid of mercury. After all the dirt possible has been separated from it mercury is mixed with the residuum and the lot stirred and mixed until the mercury has taken up all the gold, dissolving it into an amalgam of both metals. This is retorted; that is, held over a fire till the heat sublimates the mercury and leaves a mass of a light yellow, friable-looking stuff, which is the gold with more or less of the mercury still in it. It appeared that the gold in the two claims sold was so fine that it could only be saved by mercury, and the owners, with all their cunning, were shortsighted enough to break up their amalgam with which to salt the shaft. There is so much difference in appearance between amalgam, no matter how finely powdered it may be, and native dust gold, that none but those entirely ignorant in these matters could mistake one for the other; especially under a good magnifier.

A few days after my arrival in Ottawa, December, 1897, a gentleman calling himself Alexander

WORK DONE ON THE CREEKS

McDonald came to me, professing to be commissioned by the authorities at Washington to acquire information and advice regarding some work the United States was going to do along the International Boundary Line in the interior; and incidentally also to learn just how claims were marked, designated, recorded, title issued, and everything else connected with them, including copies of the printed forms used, and a copy of the signatures of all the officials connected with the Record and Title. His story seemed a strange one, and as no intimation had been sent from Washington announcing him, it looked suspicious. He produced an introductory letter from the Survey Office at Washington, and others from several important men in the United States, which he, however, did not let me examine too closely. When asked why advance letters had not been sent, he started to explain, but like the parrot in the story of the cat and dog fight, he talked too d—d much. An inquiry wire was sent to Washington, but he must have had a pal in the office at New York, for he was notified of the inquiry and our message was held there till he had time to get away. His message was handed to him in the hotel office, and when he read it, he walked out to the nearest railroad station, where he found a train just leaving, and went on it. His hotel bill is still unpaid, I believe, but his trunks and grips are security for it.

In the following April he turned up in London, England, with many valuable claims for sale. I was there at the time, but unknown to him. When asked to get from me an endorsement of the value placed by him on his property, he left for the Continent, and I had to publish an exposure of the man and his methods.

While I was in London at that time, an investigation in the matter of a sale of a fictitious claim was held. The name, "Yellow Jacket," the title, description, and value of the claim all were imaginary, but looked good enough to bring six thousand pounds (nearly thirty thousand dollars) to the author. I showed clearly enough, I thought, in my evidence that there could not be any such claim in the locality ascribed to it; further, that the size of the claim was not permitted by our regulations, and that the forms for title used were not the regular forms. Because there was a quartz claim located and recorded just across the river from Dawson, which *might* be the "Yellow Jacket," the action was dismissed. I mention these things as part of the aftermath of a great gold discovery.

CHAPTER XII

LOCAL EXCITEMENT AS THE WEALTH OF KLONDIKE WAS REVEALED

DURING the preceding summer it seemed that Fortymile Camp was exhausted, the known ground was all filled to overflowing, and no new fields were in sight. Many new adventurers were coming to the country, as well as many who had tried it before. At Fortymile inquiries, and sometimes search, soon showed that there was not much hope either of their doing anything or getting anything there, and they soon passed on down the river to the next camp, Circle City, from where, after repeating the experience at Fortymile, they passed to the next, and so on to the mouth of the river, and from there home if they had the means. Some of them, even without means, found their way back to the old home, many only to be lured back the following season by the strangely delightful wander they had had down the great river of the north, a wander once over the pass, made with so little effort, and through so strange scenes, that it was, I think, often repeated to prove whether or not the first time had been only a dream. Some also left Fortymile who had come to the end of their job or worked out their ground, and many, because they had not saved a fortune as some others had done, cast the dust from off their feet, as it were, against the place, rating it very low indeed, and vowing never to darken its landscape again with their presence; wherein they proved poor prophets. Among these pilgrims were some who had staked in the new field, the Klondike, and failing to secure a few dollars for their title had gone off, never expecting that any more would come of the venture than what followed a great many stampedes—a rush, a commotion, a revulsion, and a look out for the next.

In the fall when good pay was discovered, and claim after claim not only followed with good prospects, but beat the best, and so on till men's eyes began to protrude, and their tongues fail to express their surprise, some of the would-be knowing ones tried to steal a march on fortune by quietly leaving Fortymile for Circle City; just a friendly visit, you know, to see how things were down there, and maybe pick up for a trifle a claim or two. But maybe they didn't. Mystery was in the frozen air; and as much of it was native to Circle City as came from Fortymile. The Fortymilers did not know much about the new field. Oh, no! In fact, when they left, there was not much to know, they believed there were a few men working, and maybe it would be a paying field; but!—well—you know there is a lot of risk about those things! and so forth, and so on. But the Circle Cityites were not in a hurry about their property, maybe they would go up in the spring and look into it. So the friendly visitors returned after accomplishing little more than a visit, and arousing suspicions regarding the value of the new field, which was not yet named Klondike. A good many of those who had gone from Fortymile the preceding summer were still at Circle City waiting for something to turn up. Many of them left Fortymile with anything but friendly feelings for the district, criticizing the place, the officials, and especially the mining regulations, which exacted a recording fee of fifteen dollars, and limited the dimensions of placer claims to five hundred feet in length, and the width of the valley bottom, as against a recording fee in Alaska of two or three dollars—whatever the community of miners at the place made it—and a claim thirteen hundred and twenty feet square. Many of them, even Canadians and Britishers, called their change of residence going back to "God's Country"; however, when it dawned on them that the new field was something so rich that the reputation of the region was made, they discovered that "God's Country" might take in places other than where they were, and they resolved to confer the blessing of their presence on the new ground. It was rumoured that before leaving Circle City they held a mass meeting, and resolved: "That the conditions in it required attention to bring them in line with the most modern civilization: That in the opinion of the resolutors the claims in the new ground were much too large: That one hundred feet square of the ground in the new area was enough for any man who had the fear of God and love of his fellow-man in his heart." I have reason to believe that there was good foundation for this report, though it may have been exaggerated as I heard it. However, arrivals from Circle City were numerous through nearly all the months of February, March, and as much of April as was safe for travelling; but when they reached Dawson they found but little inclination on the part of the claim owners to accept their communistic theories, and so they had to be content with searching for fractions, that is over plus of measurement in the claims already owned and worked. Some of them had conscience enough to be ashamed of this, and it was said they did it with the aid of lanterns in the small hours of the night. One North of Ireland man, who was most pronounced in his references to "God's Country" when he left Fortymile a few months before,

LOCAL EXCITEMENT

sought diligently for a fraction in the rich parts of Bonanza and Eldorado, and at last staked one of about five feet, which he considered would be plenty for his wants if he only got it, but the survey reduced it to between three and four inches, and he left for " God's Country " again, expressing great disgust to me that a man could not get " a futt o' groun' in his own counthry." Yet he, it was alleged, while in American territory, was most violent in his denunciation of Canadians and Britishers, and was opposed to their being recognized in any way there. There were a few such cases, and it is gratifying to be able to record that when they *had* to come to the Klondike they were extended very little sympathy by either Canadians, Britishers, or Americans. One American was fortunate enough to secure a large fraction on Bonanza Creek near discovery claim, and realized a large fortune out of it. It was well known as the Lowe fraction. It was eighty-six feet in depth, by some three hundred feet wide across the valley, and cleaned up about four hundred thousand dollars. Few richer bits of ground have been found anywhere.

ESTIMATES OF GREAT VALUES NOT OVERDRAWN

While I was making the survey I frequently got data from claim owners showing what they were doing, and how the ground worked, "prospected" (that is the average value per pan in gold). From the known area of the claim as I found it I made computations to determine how the ground so tested would yield, and found it surprisingly rich. On one claim in particular, number sixteen on Eldorado, owned by Mr. Thomas Lippy, now of Seattle, the data furnished me by him pointed to a final output of a million and a half dollars. In other cases the figures ran to about a million. From all the data furnished me in this way, I came to the conclusion that there were at least sixty claims on Bonanza Creek and forty on Eldorado that would average not less than one thousand dollars per running foot, and the assertion was often severely criticized and ridiculed. One gentleman while lecturing in Ottawa, who had just come from the Klondike, while acknowledging my ability as an astronomer, doubted my capacity to make the calculation which authorized this assertion. He did not know that any schoolboy, if given the data furnished me, could make the calculation as well as the greatest mathematician alive; it was simply the superficial area of the claim, which I knew, multiplied by the depth in feet of the pay gravel, and the result multiplied by five, the average number of pans in a foot, and you have the number of pay pans in the

KLONDIKERS MUSHING OVER DYEA PASS, 1898

claim. The claim owner gave me the average value of a pan, which, multiplied by the number of pans, is the presumptive output in dollars; very simple. I had the gratification in the fall of 1904 of meeting Mr. Lippy's foreman, who told me the claim had just been worked out, and my estimate had been exceeded by a little over thirty thousand dollars. I also, about the same time, had the gratification of having an acquaintance of several years, whom I met in Dawson, remark: " I want to shake hands with you, Mr. Ogilvie, and congratulate you at the same time." " I am glad to shake hands with you, but do not understand the congratulation," I replied. " Well, I heard you in London in 1898 make e statement publicly that there were one hundred million dollars in sight in the Klondike region, and at least another hundred millions, probably two of them, to be discovered. I laughed at the time, and called you an old granny who did not know what she was talking about; well, your hundred millions and more are out now; and as for what is left, my own estimate, based on a great deal of testing, is that it is much more than you said."

I mention this because it has often been said that my excessive estimates of the gold in the Klondike were directly responsible for the royalty tax imposed on the output of the mines by the Dominion Government. The fact is that no estimates of mine became public until after the royalty had been imposed; but even had I known that the imposition of a royalty would follow any statement of mine, and I had as good reason to make it, as I knew at the time I had, and time has since justified, I would have made it all the same. As to my reports to the Department, I could not begin to make any of positive value regarding the new fields till June, 1897. In November, 1896, there was an opportunity to send out a letter by Capt. Moore, who has before been mentioned. He had come down the river with the last of his three mails about the middle of September, and as he had arranged to deliver the American mail, he intended to continue down-stream to the mouth of the river, and go by steamer from there to Seattle, thence home. The storm that kept me in the country held up the veteran riverman also; he had to provide himself with a dog team, and walking and riding as the state of the roads permitted, this man, in his seventy-third year, made his way from Circle City to Fortymile, where he spent a day or two repairing sled and harness, when the journey was resumed to Dawson, where he switched off up Bonanza and staked a claim, resuming the outward journey up the river, and made his way safely out, in the bitter winter weather

LOCAL EXCITEMENT

over roads, or rather no roads at all, that would have to be seen to be realized. A week or so before the Captain left Fortymile a party of three young men, all apparently fit to battle for their lives, started out with much flourish of banners and blare of trumpets. They were going to make a record trip out, and they did. The Captain overhauled them all nearly broken down, almost out of provisions, and very dispirited. He took them along with him, and landed the whole party safe at Juneau. I sent out with him a short report, telling what I could learn of the new discovery; but at that time, with the exception of one or two claims on Bonanza, not much of a positive character was known. About January 21st, 1897, Thomas W. O'Brien, a pioneer, started for the outside; and a few days after Stewart Menzies, in the employ of the Alaska Commercial Company, left with dispatches for his company. I sent out short reports with those gentlemen, and was able to say that the new camp gave much promise of being the greatest yet established in the territory, and probably would prove worldstartling. No further opportunity offered itself to send mail till the middle of June, when, as I was making my way up to Selkirk with a heavily loaded canoe, two men passed me outward bound. They were light, and travelling fast. I hailed them, and asked if they would take out a letter for me, which they agreed to do. Sitting on the bank of the Yukon, I wrote on my knee a short letter to the Minister of the Interior, saying I was very pleased to be able to assure him that my most sanguine expectations respecting the new camp were more than realized by results, both as to the extent and quality. I told him that from extensive and exact observations I had been able to make in the field, I estimated the output for that season to be about two and a half million dollars. I did not again report till I did so personally in September.

CHAPTER XIII

EXPERIENCES IN CAMP AND ON RIVER

AFTER the survey of the claims, and some work at Selkirk, I remained at Dawson, awaiting a boat for St. Michael, which did not come until the middle of July. Meanwhile Mr. Thomas Fawcett, having been appointed Gold Commissioner, arrived with his clerk, Mr. Robert Bryce Craig. The office was opened in Dawson, and the work thus transferred from Fortymile to the vicinity of the mines.

During the winter the last arrival from the outside who brought any newspapers, brought dire intelligence indeed. According to the papers, Queen Victoria was critically ill; Pope Leo XIII was at the point of death; war was imminent between England and Russia; and, more exciting to the camp, a fight for the championship of the world was coming off some time in the spring between the star pugilists, James J. Corbett and Robert FitzSimmons. All were sorry for the " poor old Queen," as it was expressed, and much sympathy was shown;

all regretted the passing away of the Pope; great anxiety prevailed about the war; and nearly everybody bet on the fight, the Americans to a man on Corbett, the old-country people on "Fitz," as he was called, even when they were doubtful if he would win, while the Canadians divided their allegiance. Imagine five or six hundred people receiving this news late in January, and not learning any more till May. In the camp was an individual who was known as Lawyer ———, because he had been a lawyer's clerk for a time, and at miners' meetings generally told the multitude what the law was, clothing it after the fashion of the cloth in Norman-French and Latin terms. Now this man at times put things very pithily; in epigrams it might be said. At noon May 14th, 1897, the ice in the river began to run, and ran full till the morning of the 16th, when it thinned out enough for boats to come down; and they came! At that time the town site of Dawson was covered with scrub timber, with a fringe of larger trees along the riverbank. On the south side of the Klondike River was a few acres of flat just below a rock-cliff on the bank of the Yukon. This had been built on by the Indians, and their cabins had been bought by some of the white men in the country. Two of the cabins were, at the time I speak of, occupied as saloons. Joe Ladue had a saloon, the only one in Dawson. There was a little whisky in the place and a good deal of water, but the boys, for the sake of old times, were willing to pay fifty cents a glass for the mixture. The hamlet south of the Klondike is now known as South Dawson, but its name then was not dignified, and was bestowed on it by the Dawsonites in contempt. It was called after a small insect that is not permitted about the person or premises of cleanly people. Now the saloon-keepers of this hamlet were wise in their day and generation, also, they were human in so far that they were resentful because of the slight put on their town, and determined to show that even the lowliest may be vengeful, so they painted a large sign, " Danger Below. Keep to the Right," and put it on high poles at a prominent point nearly a mile above their town. Now the first boats of the Klondike rush were following the ice down as closely as possible, and in the early morning of May 16th, when they saw this sign, they naturally were alarmed, and at once hugged the right bank as closely as possible, till they came to the first town. Here they all landed and proceeded to inquire about things, and also answer questions, at the same time drinking occasional glasses of whisky and water. They assumed they were at Dawson, and there was no one there to impress them differently. It happened that morning that Lawyer —— had gone over the Klondike from Dawson to the other place, where he saw the beach literally covered with boats. It was no part of his duty to spoil business, so he drank the visitors' whisky, but did not tell them there was another, and a much larger Dawson, even if it had only one saloon. After some time spent with the incomers, and they were still coming, he returned. No sooner had he landed than he proceeded to tell the good news of the arrivals. I was standing some distance away, but thought I heard him say something about boats, and raised my voice to a shout, and asked him about it. He replied that a good many boats had come down behind the thick ice, had landed at L—e town, and were there yet. I asked, " How many ? "

" About two hundred."

" How many people ? "

" About six hundred."

" Well, what's the news ? "

" *The Pope's alive! The Queen's well! There's no war! and Bob FitzSimmons knocked h—l out of Jim Corbett!* "

That was all, and it was all we were anxious about for months. Imagine it on a newspaper bulletin board. As soon as Joe Ladue heard of this influx, and that it was drinking up all the whisky in the camp of the enemy, he was wroth, and swore mightily. How to get the multitude to come and partake of his hospitality was a serious matter to him. I offered to get them down if he would let me have the use of his sawmill, which was running. He accepted, and I tied the steam-whistle open. The continuous blast caused inquiry, satisfactory answers were not given, and soon the rush to Dawson was on. A wilderness of tents covered the ground, without regard to order or convenience. Every hour of every day boats of all patterns and designs arrived, each with several occupants The Gold Commissioner's Office was henceforth a veritable hive of industry for more hours in the day than offices are generally held open.

When I reached St. Michael late in July I found crowds there waiting for a steamer on which to make their way up. I was compelled to remain for some time waiting for a steamship south bound, and the experience was certainly unique. But few of the multitudes Klondike bound had any idea of even where it was, or the climatic, political, or judicial conditions existing there. The passengers of one steamer, after due deliberation, resolved themselves into a committee of the whole to devise ways and means of preserving order when they should reach the camp, and the committee of the whole appointed itself a vigilance committee after the manner of something they had read somewhere in some story of the west. Learning that

I, a person who had spent some time at the camp, had just come down, they sought me. I listened for some time to the verbal report they made to me of their actions, and their intentions regarding the preservation of law and good order. I then told them that their interference would be quite unnecessary, that the North-West Mounted Police would attend to law, and order, and everything else necessary. They wanted to know what the North-West Mounted Police was, and when I explained, they inquired who sent them there. When told that it was the Canadian Government, they wanted to know what in —— the Canadian Government had to do with it, and it took some time, and some references to maps I had, to convince them the diggings were in Canada. I met many reporters sent specially to the new camp for this, that, or the other newspaper. Many of these got long interviews from me and turned back. I had hundreds of photograph negatives with me, from which I made many prints for the reporters, and they appeared in due time as having been taken specially for " our journal," though no one belonging to the journal had ever been within a thousand miles of the scenes ; indeed, it would have taken a whole season to visit them, for I had been gathering them for two years and a half. Major Ray and Captain Richardson, of the United States Army, were at St. Michael while I was there. They had been sent by the United States Government to spend the winter in Alaska, to attend to the preservation of law and order as much as possible, and to inquire into the conditions and requirements of the country, with a view to a regular military establishment later on.

Major Ray held several conferences with me regarding the region I had just spent two years in, and was most anxious to learn everything of practical value connected with the whole northern region. Both he and Captain Richardson impressed me as eminently fair and practical in their views.

THE ROYALTY TAX

At St. Michael I learned of the changes in the mining regulations, and the imposition of the royalty tax.

A few words relating to this tax will not be out of place here, more especially as to the why and the when it was imposed.

The *why*, I may say, was more the exaggerated reports of the western newspapers than any other thing. I had reported that the output for the season of 1897 would be two and a half million dollars, which was not far from the truth. But when the reports created for the Press, one after the other, reached Eastern Canada, they created great excitement, as it was intended they should everywhere. When the total output, according to these gross exaggerations, reached nearly twenty millions, and all that flowing into the United States, the people of Eastern Canada very naturally took the matter up, and were strongly of opinion that Canada should derive some benefit. If I am not very much mistaken, strong pressure was brought to bear on the Minister to do something to secure to Canada a share of the vast sums taken from its treasure field into strange countries. Other countries forbade such a condition by preventing aliens from securing mining claims in their territory. Canada, in accordance with British precedent, did not do this, so another way had to be tried to benefit by the richness of her fields. As a sample of the way reports were manufactured, I may cite the case of the ship on which I went to San Francisco at the time of which I speak. One of the owners was aboard, and he knew a great deal about the financial condition of most of the passengers. He knew positively how much gold belonging to his company was aboard. Jack McQuesten was also with us, and what he did not know about the passengers was not worth knowing. I also knew considerable about them and their wealth. We canvassed the boat, and learned positively that the total in dust aboard was five hundred and eighty-seven thousand dollars. We were sure to within a couple

EXPERIENCES IN CAMP

of thousand dollars of the truth. When we reached San Francisco we had not got through the Golden Gate before tugs with reporters met us; went through the passengers, and found two and a half millions on them. A list was then published, and opposite every name was set a sum, the whole aggregating the amount stated. Poor Mr. Harper, who came down to die, was credited with sixty thousand; he had not a cent, being dependent at the time on the Alaska Commercial Company. There were other similar cases, and I, to escape the annoyance of several long interviews, had arranged to pass as one of the crew, thus losing, I have no doubt, great credit for dust. The public believed in the two and a half millions, and so acted.

In the last days of September, at Vancouver, B.C., I met Mr. Sifton, the Minister of the Interior, Major Walsh, the newly appointed Commissioner of the Yukon Territory, and the staff of officials appointed to accompany him to Dawson, and returned north with them to Tagish, on the lake of that name. I learned then that a handbook of information concerning the Klondike and Yukon generally had been prepared by one of the clerks in the Department of the Interior, and that it had a very wide circulation. Though the clerk took great pains to make it reliable, he was personally unacquainted with the country he was dealing with, and naturally some of his inferences and impressions were not quite correct. I mention this because I have often been taxed with getting up the book. I did not reach Ottawa until the middle of December, and as soon as possible set about writing an official guide or handbook for the benefit of intending Klondikers. This work did not go through the press till the last days of January, 1898, so thousands who thought they had my book never saw it. While preparing it I was deluged with inquiries about every conceivable thing regarding the Klondike region, and a myriad of inconceivable things as well.

CHAPTER XIV

METHODS OF MINING

I WILL now describe the methods of mining in vogue in the early days, and compare them with those of more recent date.

We have already seen that the first mining done in the territory was confined to the bars and banks of the streams, for the reason that it was considered impossible to reach bed-rock as in other regions, where less frost prevailed. In those days the principal means of separating the fine gold from the sand and gravel was the rocker. In all the methods used a common principle existed; that is, the principle of gravity. Gold is nineteen times heavier than water, and seven to eight times heavier than rock, and although native gold is never pure, consequently lighter than pure, the difference does not affect the principle of extraction. Generally, then, the practical application of the principle to the separation of the precious metal from the dirt holding it, is an inclined plane, over which a stream of water is made to flow. The gold-bearing dirt is shovelled into the fast-flowing stream, which carries along the lighter material and leaves the heavy gold behind. To aid in arresting and holding the gold, barriers are put in the bottom of the trough. Where there is plenty of water, and a head can be had, that is, if the water can be taken from a higher level to a lower one, a series of troughs are made of plank, as wide as possible consistent with the supply of water. These are elevated on trestles or other appliances, so that the water enters the high end and flows through them. They are fitted into each other at the joints, so that the stream is continuous, and the line of three or more " sluice boxes," as they are termed, is sloped, to give the water momentum enough to carry down the gravel and sand, yet hardly move the gold. The progress of the metal is finally stopped by the barriers, called " riffles." These are in up-to-date gold-saving plants made of angle iron, cut into lengths the width of the sluice box, and bolted together at a constant distance from each other, in groups resembling a large gridiron. The groups are, of course, limited in size for convenience in handling. Sometimes, especially when the gold is fine, expanded metal and coco-matting are associated with the riffles. The metal is laid on top of the matting, so that its bars throw down the fine material and the gold is entrapped in the matting. The bars of angle iron in the riffles

BANANZA VALLEY SHORTLY AFTER A STRIKE, 1896

METHODS OF MINING

are set about an inch apart. The spaces soon fill with sand and fine gravel, but the small cataract formed by the water falling over each bar keeps a basin between them in which the gold and heavy material remains, the heavier bits at the top, and the lighter scattered along in proportion to their size and weight; and the very lightest in the coco-matting. In the early days the riffles were made of bars of wood, generally sections of small trees, cut in convenient lengths, placed parallel to each other, and held in that position by a section of plank nailed on to their ends. These sections of riffles, unlike those made of angle iron, were placed longitudinally with the sluice box, instead of transversely. That system is all right where the gold is very coarse, but with fine gold a lot of it escapes. Small stones soon got wedged between the wooden bars, and pits in the sand were formed between them, as in the case of the angle-iron bars. Variations of the sluice box and riffles constitute all the methods of washing gold. Where the sluice box could be used, it always was, but it is obvious that on bar and bank mining there would be but few places where the miner could avail himself of it, and those only where a stream joining the main one came in with a rapid descent. Generally the fall in the box had to be about one in four or five to get the best results, so that in thirty feet of box there had to be a head, or drop, of five to seven feet. The sluice box enabled the operator to work a great deal more dirt than by any other system of manual labour. The material was simply thrown into the head of the line of boxes, the water did the rest. Bringing the dirt to the box was the greatest part of the labour.

Where the sluice box could not be utilized for lack of a head of water the rocker had to be employed. As its name implies, it is a box some three or four feet in length, and twenty to twenty-four inches wide, placed on a pair of rockers, such as might be found on an old-fashioned household cradle. On top of this box a shallow box or hopper with a thin iron-plate bottom was placed. The iron plate was plentifully punched with quarter-inch holes. Below this cover was one or more sloping shelves, covered with a bit of blanket or, in some cases, a small riffle. Close beside a stream or pool of water, two hewed blocks were firmly fixed in the ground, and on these the rockers of the machine were placed. The operator took his place beside the rocker with a long-handled dipper in one hand, and the other ready to rock. If alone, he first filled the shallow box with fine gravel, rejecting all the coarse parts. He then ladled water on to the mass, at the same time rocking the machine from side to side; the water and motion combined carried the finer and heavier parts of the sand and gravel through the holes in the iron plate, and they fell on to the inclined shelves below, down which they were sluiced by the water, the gold being caught by the wool of the blanket or in the riffles, as the case might be. If two or more persons were working in partnership, one carried gravel and loaded the hopper, while the other rocked. Several times a day the blankets or riffles were taken out and washed in a tub of water to get the gold out of them. They were then replaced and the work resumed. This process, it is evident, is slow and laborious, but there were many places where it was the only method available. By it a pair of men could clean from one and a half to four cubic yards per day. With sluice boxes and a plentiful supply of water, many times that quantity could be washed. When we reflect that two men by this method averaged about one hundred dollars per day on the bars of Stewart River, we can form some idea of the richness of the ground they worked. When we are told that six men during a little more than two months took out by this tedious, laborious process about thirty-five thousand dollars from one of the famous bars of that stream, it surprises us. But when we recollect that at many other places along the banks and bars of the Yukon and Hootalinqua men were making very good wages by this process when the discovery of coarse gold on Fortymile put a period to bar and bank diggings, we can form some estimate of the future of the region when dredge and other approved methods of mining such ground, under the conditions existing there, are installed on the scale the region justifies.

As we have seen, firing the bars in the early spring months during the period of the very lowest water, to get the richer parts of the deposits, which were inaccessible in summer, led to firing or thawing to bed-rock. This gave a tremendous advance to mining in this hitherto " skim " mining region, as it was considered. It opened regions of ground before thought impossible, and made room for scores where one had been considered enough. Vast improvement as it was, it was very expensive and wasteful of fuel. The fire was not confined, it could not be, to produce the best result. Naturally ascending, the heat thawed a great deal more ground than held pay, and this had to be handled with the rest, greatly reducing the average per yard of the dirt worked, and at the same time increasing the cost of working in the same ratio. The pay streak was often not more than three feet in depth, and the burning thawed seven, eight, and nine feet. During the winter of 1897 much discussion was held by the miners concerning the improvement of the firing method. All sorts of ways were proposed,

METHODS OF MINING

only to be dropped after thorough examination; but two stood out prominently and permanently, namely, thawing by steam, and thawing by coal oil or gasolene flames. The latter idea was an enlarged plumber's torch, the intense flame of which was to be directed against the wall of frozen earth. Of the two, the steam was considered the most adequate, but the gasolene torch was more portable, involving no boiler or wood; the cost of the gasolene or oil, however, at that time—and yet—one dollar per gallon, was prohibitive, no matter what the practical merit of the method might prove; and though wood became more and more scarce, it never got high enough in cost to reach the level of the gasolene. The gasolene torch was tried, but its action was too slow and too local. Steam at a pressure of about forty pounds to the inch was carried in flexible hose, and applied through "points," that is, a section of half-inch iron pipe five or six feet long, into one end of which a steel plug is inserted. In this are bored two or three holes one-eighth of an inch in diameter, through which the steam issues against the frozen gravel, and thaws it at an astonishing rate. The points were held against the wall till driven into it their full length, and were then left to do their work. This process did a great deal more work with the same amount of wood, and, better still, the limits of the work were much more under control. With improved hoisting machinery, better sluice boxes and riffles, ground could be worked with good profit that would not be touched in the earlier years of the territory. At one time the minimum value worked was ten cents to the pan, now less than a fourth of that is eagerly sought.

HYDRAULICKING

So far hydraulicking, as carried on in California and elsewhere, has not been extensively tested, and whether that method can be utilized profitably is not decided yet. There are, no doubt, places where it will prove practicable and profitable, but the almost universal condition of frozen ground, to as yet undetermined depth, is a handicap too serious to be dismissed by a hope that it will come all right anyway. Generally, where it might be applied with advantage, a good head of water, which is the essential feature of the system, is difficult and expensive to get, and this bars all attempts at the method unless they are backed by very large amounts of money. One company is now engaged in bringing water to the hillsides of the Klondike at an expense of several millions of dollars. The work has been going on for several years, and will not be completed for one or two more. That the field to be operated justifies the expenditure

METHODS OF MINING 233

of time and money there seems to be no doubt, and I am sure the friends of the Klondike heartily hope so.

DREDGING

Dredging was first thought of as a mode of developing some of the ground in the winter of 1898. While I was in London a syndicate which owned a valuable piece of ground in the Klondike consulted me about putting a dredge on it. After every aspect of the question had been thrashed out, it was decided that though the method would very likely prove the best under all the circumstances, the machine would have to enter via the St. Michael route, and so reach Dawson too late the first season to do more than arrange to have it hauled by sleighs to the field, where most of the work of putting together the machinery would have to be done; this coming in, in parts small enough to be handled by men. This, together with the enormous freight rates of that time, would pile up the cost of even a medium capacity machine to a practically prohibitive sum, and the idea was abandoned, never to be taken up again by the same persons. In the summer of 1898 a personal friend of my own, the late Mr. John A. McPherson, who was associated with a Cincinnati capitalist, Mr. Hines, brought the machinery and lumber for the construction of a small dredge over the White Pass Railway, which had just been completed, to the head of Lake Bennet, and from there by the Cañon route to the leaseholds owned by them on the Lewes River, extending some distance above the mouth of the Big Salmon. Notwithstanding all the difficulties confronting Mr. McPherson, the material was all safely landed, the hull constructed, launched, machinery erected, and the dredge at work the first week in September, which is something of a record. As is usual in such ventures, under new and largely unknown conditions, it took all the remainder of the season to get the machine adjusted to its environment. Mr. McPherson was on his way back to the field the following spring, but he met with a serious accident on the coast, and had to return to his home after a stay in the hospital. His associate, Mr. Hines, came in, but after running the dredge for a short time near Big Salmon River, he was, I was informed, taken sick, and becoming disheartened, ordered the machine down-stream to be sold or returned to the builders. At Dawson it was arranged with some parties there to place it on one of the claims on lower Bonanza. It was dismantled and hauled by wagon to claim No. 42 below discovery, where it was set up, and though the ground was frozen from the surface down to bed-rock, it worked it out in less than two seasons,

METHODS OF MINING

with profit to both machine owners and claim owners. It was then moved up to discovery claim, which it worked over again after it was worked out by the hand system. The ground here was thawed by steam to save wear and tear of the dredge and increase its output, and though this is expensive, it was continued, showing that it must have paid. The owners of the dredge also purchased from our friend Skookum Jim the remains of his claim, No. 1 above discovery, after he had worked on it about six years, paying for it sixty thousand dollars, which shows, perhaps, more forcibly than anything else that could be said, the thoroughness of dredging as compared with the old system of firing and sluicing, by which Jim principally worked.

Two steam shovels were put to work in the Klondike valley near the mouth of Bear Creek, some four miles above the mouth of the Klondike. The ground was very good, and the method paid, but a dredge replaced them two years later. In 1902 a small dredge was put on the Stewart to test the gravels there. It operated part of two seasons, and though poorly suited to the work, its results have been the cause of two other dredges of up-to-date design and capacity being put on that stream, and the intention apparently is to add to the number till a fleet of not fewer than ten is working. There are several working in the Klondike valley, and also in the Bonanza valley, placed there since 1904. The Bonanza ones are, it is said, working out the valley bottom, preparatory to the hillsides being washed into it, when the arrangements for bringing water for that purpose are completed. In the beds of the large streams the gravels are not frozen, so these huge machines can work up to their full capacity, some of them to four and five thousand cubic yards per day of twenty-four hours. But away from the flowing waters the frost has bound the ground firmly, and the output of the machines is very limited, and the wear and tear of the buckets very great. It is possible that by working a large pool for each dredge, and heating the water and keeping it circulating, or even circulating it alone, the trouble with frost will be very much reduced. There is no doubt that, as time goes on, new ways and methods of combating this great handicap of the north will be developed. It is mainly the coming means of working the treasure out of a large part of the area there, and it is only a question of human ingenuity, which always conquers, to meet the difficulties and offset them. The machines themselves are constantly being improved to meet new conditions, and there is no doubt that they will conquer in this field, as well as in all the others into which they have entered.

METHODS OF MINING 237

Dredging, like hydraulicking, requires a lot of money to begin it properly, so much that it cannot be counted available to any but the wealthy or a company. A medium-sized machine when put to work in the most accessible parts of the Yukon Territory will cost from sixty to seventy-five thousand dollars. A larger one will cost proportionally more, depending on the weight of metal in the machinery and the amount of lumber in the hull and house. Something, too, depends on the quality of metal in the working parts. It is safe to state that a machine, of say 250 cubic yards' capacity per hour, not a very large one as they go now, will cost not less than one hundred thousand dollars in the most advantageously situated parts of the Yukon Territory, that is at points on the main tributaries, like the Hootalinqua, Pelly, or Stewart, or even on the main stream itself. If the material has to be hauled far from the main arteries, the cost may be doubled or even trebled, depending on the distance and difficulties. It is very evident then that the prospector has not much show to make anything by this method, unless he is prepared to give the lion's share to some one who will provide a dredge. Here, too, he is handicapped by the regulations which require the payment of one hundred dollars per mile of river bed, sixty days after his application is filed. He is allowed to acquire ten miles, and has to pay down one thousand dollars. He is required to put on a dredge to be approved by the Minister of the Interior within three years of the issuance of his lease, and to pay ten dollars per mile each subsequent year of the existence of his leasehold. Now it will take more than one season to thoroughly prospect the ground, and if he begins prospecting before making application, he is at the mercy of any one who may deem it good enough to acquire. The sixty days after application will hardly enable one to get the necessary appliances for prospecting to the ground. The drill alone required to make the necessary tests will cost about three thousand dollars laid down at White Horse, and take a month to get there, and it may cost nearly as much and take more time to get it from there to the ground desired. After the ground is selected, all that can be done in the sixty days between the date of application and the payment of the money is to make a very superficial examination which may be very misleading in its results; the prospects on the surface being good, but nothing beneath, there is no way to tell differently till a drill has thoroughly and systematically prospected the leasehold from surface to bed-rock, unless the latter should prove to be at an impracticable depth, in which case the test would have to be limited to a practical digging depth for a dredge.

METHODS OF MINING

This depth may be modified by conditions that can be learned only through the work of the drill. The minimum width allowed for a dredging stream is one hundred and fifty feet, all under that being reserved for placer mining. Let us assume that we have a leasehold ten miles long, and varying from two to three hundred feet wide. Such a stretch of ground ought to have at least a pair of drill holes at intervals of five hundred feet, and this would not give a too conclusive test. Under the most favourable circumstances two holes a week would be good work, which takes into consideration moving the drill, and all other contingencies. Ten miles would require in this not too critical examination two hundred and ten holes, which would take one hundred weeks, and as the most favourable season there affords not more than twenty-two, we see that it would require five seasons to complete the prospect, and the applicant has to go it blind altogether too much. True he may have learned from other sources something of the nature of the locality he is in, but in the case of a pioneer, or pioneers, that is not likely.

I would suggest that the applicant, after sixty days, be required to pay down, say ten per cent of the purchase money, and as soon as practically possible begin comprehensive, systematic prospecting work. I say *as soon as possible*, because what would be possible in one place there would be absolutely impossible in another, and if the country is to be developed, we must take possibilities, and especially impossibilities, into account. The Territorial Mining Engineer, or some other competent official in the territory, could easily decide just what was and what was not possible in each case. As soon as a sufficient portion of the leasehold was prospected, and if the tests showed values sufficient to justify it, the installation of a dredge should be required in a practicable time, the engineer or other official again reporting as to the desirability of the machine, basing his requirements on the sworn returns of the prospector from the work he has done (verified personally where possible by the engineer, or some one for him), and on the situation of the leasehold. Should all the ground not prove paying, the privilege of abandoning the unprofitable portion to be permitted, and the balance of the hundred dollars per mile retained to be paid. This would not involve the risk of the miner losing his money, and would prevent dishonest speculation with poor or worthless ground. A few words showing the relative burdens imposed on the placer miner and the dredger will not be out of place. A placer mine is five hundred feet in length, along the creek or gulch, and two thousand feet in width, thus containing very nearly

WIND-DRIVEN SLEDS ON TAKU RIVER, 1895-96

twenty-three acres. The recording fee is ten dollars per annum, and the regulations require two hundred dollars' worth of work to be performed on the claim every season. The methods by which this work may be done are laid down in the local regulations, and certainly they are liberal enough; any one who wishes can do the work with very little trouble. It can easily be done in a month by one man. Take a dredging leasehold of ten miles in length, and an average width of three hundred feet, which contains three hundred and sixty-three and two-third acres, the recording fee is one thousand dollars for the first year, and one hundred for each subsequent one. In the case of the placer claim it is at the rate of forty-four cents per acre, and for the first year in the case of the dredging lease two dollars and seventy-five cents per acre, and one-tenth of that for all other years. The representation work on a placer claim—two hundred dollars per year—is equivalent to eight dollars and seventy cents per acre, while the representation work on a dredging lease, exclusive of prospecting, which, as we have seen, is absolutely necessary, is for the first three years a dredge which to be of reasonably good service must cost at least seventy-five thousand dollars before a wheel is turned, and probably will be double that; anyway, it is not less than twenty-five thousand per year for the first three years, or nearly seventy dollars per acre. Afterwards, the running expenses and wear and tear of the dredge will average seventy-five to one hundred dollars per day, during a season of about one hundred and fifty days.

In the case of a quartz claim, which is allowed fifteen hundred feet square, or fifty-one and two-third acres, it is acquired by planting and marking three stakes, paying a recording fee of five dollars, performing one hundred dollars' worth of work per year on it for five years, when, upon filing a plan and description of survey, a patent deed may be obtained for it by paying one dollar per acre; and the land is for ever the property of the patentee, without power of interference from any one. These conditions are decidedly easy. It might be said that dredging is the capitalist's method of mining, and he can afford to pay for what he gets. That argument, if valid at all, will apply with almost equal force to the quartz miner, for he, too, requires a lot of money to establish himself properly.

If the dredger could be accorded some consideration in the way of assurance that he will not lose his ground, and all the labour performed on it, because he has failed to live up to the regulations, he would not have so much reason to complain. He is required to do certain

TAGISH LAKE POLICE AND CUSTOM STATION, HON. CLIFFORD SIFTON, MAJOR WALSH, AND INSPECTOR STRICKLAND STANDING TOGETHER, 1897

things every year of the life of his leasehold, and if he fails he is liable to lose all. This is in the hands of the Minister of the Interior, and we may accept it as an axiom that that gentleman will never impose any unreasonable or unnecessary hardship on any one, so long as he does the best he can under the circumstances. Good public policy would require this. There is no positive assurance, however, that he will not, as the regulations provide he may, and the doubt breeds doubt in the mind of the investor.

In the case of the quartz miner, we have seen that he can acquire absolute title. Why not provide something akin to that in the case of the dredger? It would be easy to assure him that if he failed in living up to the requirements after spending a lot of money, that an interest in the ground, proportionate to what he expended, would be given him; that would be little enough, and much less than what is given the quartz miner who, as far as development of the country goes, is entitled to no more consideration than the dredger. The future of dredging is the future of a very large area of the country, too poor or too difficult for the placer individual, and it is not unreasonable to ask consideration of the restrictions on the dredger. He should have more assurance against total loss, and a little more freedom of action.

He cannot assign or transfer his leasehold without the consent of the Minister of the Interior, while, as we have seen, the quartz-claim holder can acquire his claim absolutely, and do as he likes with it.

CHAPTER XV

ADMINISTRATION OF LAW IN EARLY CAMPS

THE judicial customs of all countries and communities, however small, have always been of interest, and those of a mining camp cannot be less so. The record of camp justice, as far as I know it, will be brought down to the advent of established judicial service in the territory in 1898. There are few who have lived anywhere contiguous to mining camps who have not heard or read of "miners' meetings." They may be called to consider any question related to the camp. In United States Territory they have a much wider scope than in Canada, as each locality makes its own by-laws, elects its recorder, fixes the amount of the recording fee, and decides the size of the claims, not to exceed thirteen hundred and twenty feet square; all of which is done in Canada by the Department of the Interior. They were also called in the case of a dispute, by one or both of the disputants, to hear the evidence and settle the matter, and it is in this capacity that I propose to speak of them. In the first days of mining in the territory when the mining groups were scattered, with but a few members in each, they were simple, fairly just, inexpensive, quick in results, and promptly executed. Can we claim all this for our more elaborate judicial machinery? In such small communities it followed that every member of it knew as much of the doings in camp as every other, and that all had a pretty accurate conception of the characteristics of the others. I may be permitted to digress here to say that it appears to me that this was the root idea from which our jury system sprang. In a small community, such as were very common in early times, it is likely that everybody knew everybody else pretty well, and it would be very difficult for false evidence to escape unchallenged, also a man's known character would avail him something in a trial. Nowadays, in some places, the object seems to be to get a jury that knows absolutely nothing about the case or its participants; and an individual in our time and generation who does not know a good deal about the matter, if not the parties to it, long before it is called, is not fit to be on a jury or any other deliberative body of citizens. When the meeting was summoned, all who could spare the time repaired to it, for all knew that some day they might be in trouble too, and if they did not manifest some interest in the camp doings, it might be a cool time for them when their trouble came. After the meeting was organized by electing a chairman and secretary, which last was generally the camp recorder, each disputant was requested to state his case, and then evidence was heard. When all was in, it was discussed openly and a vote taken, the majority carrying the judgment, which was promptly executed. At some of the meetings all this formality was not observed, but where the meeting contained experienced men it generally was. As the country filled up and the communities grew larger, results became different, from various causes; sectionalism sprang up at times, and nationalism began to crop up, but, worst of all, that potent factor in modern mischief, the saloon, began to have an influence. What time it came into the field I cannot say, but think it was about 1889. There was a big profit in whisky, and some who were going in, anyway, combined business with necessity, invested a few dollars in liquor, took it along and sold it at an enormous advance. Some found it so profitable and congenial that they took to the business almost exclusively, and were afterwards known by the name of "Whisky" prefixed to the surname, whatever it might be. The liquor was sold to the saloon-keepers, who retailed it along with some *water* at fifty cents a glass. Like the saloons everywhere else, they had their clientele of loafers, and, like all the tribe, they interfered with other people's business more than they attended to their own. After the establishment of saloons, miners' meetings were often held in them, and as all present were generally counted miners, as indeed they all were, more or less, only some were so when they had to be, seeing it was the only means of employment in the country, so all had a vote. As an instance of the kind of awards that were sometimes given at the meetings, I will cite the case of a French Canadian, known as French Joe, as told me by himself.

Joe had been up the creek for several weeks, and thought he would take a run down and see how the town, as they called Fortymile, looked. Passing a cabin he was hailed by the occupant, and asked if he was going to town, and as Joe said, " I tole 'im yes, den he hax me if I would take down a couple o' hounces an' give it to Bill Smit' for him, I tole him all right, he hax me in, and he weight de couple a hounces o' dust, an' geeve it to me. Well, sir, I take it down, an' geeve it to Smit', he weigh it an' say dat's all right, but dat son of a gun ho me tree hounces. I say I don' know what he ho you, he geeve me two hounces to geeve to you, your got it, dat's all I got to do wit' it, but he say I mus' geeve him de hudder hounce dat fellar ho him. I say I donno what he ho you, he might ho you a tousan' hounces, I don ho you noting, I geeve you de two hounces he hax me to fetch you, dat's hall I have to do wit' it. Well, sir, dat fellar call miners' meetin' hon me, in Bob Hinglish's saloon, de place was full, eighty-six man was dare; Bob was make chairman. Smit' tell de way he want it; I hax heem if he got his two hounces. He say yes. I say, well boys, dat's all I know 'bout de ting, I get two hounces to geeve him, I give it, I do'no what dat fella ho him, I got noting to do wit' it. Well, sir, dey take a vote on dat, six vote for Smit', five for me, de res' dey don't give a d—m nohow, I los' me case, I got to pay twenty dollars for de use of de saloon to hol' de meetin' on, I got to treat all hand, and go hout and borry de hudder hounce to pay, dat's cos' me more dan hundred dollars; *no, sir!* I don' want no more miners' meetin's, me." That was Joe's story, but it may have been coloured a little in the telling. I never had an opportunity to hear the other side. It was generally alleged in the camp that Joe was a social cuss, so much so that when he came to town he always had a "time," and they may have thought that he might as well spend a few dollars in the way they made him, as in his own. Whether or not a meeting held out of town would have returned such a decision, it is bootless to discuss, but of one thing we are certain, he would not have had to treat so many men at an expense of fifty cents a glass, and it is not likely, social as he may have been, that he would have found so many for himself. As was before remarked, a man's standing in the community stood him in good stead in the case of a dispute. Saloon-keepers as a rule were a hearty lot of good fellows, whose generosity was often helpful to many; nevertheless, their places were rendezvous for idlers, and often fruitful of mischief. In the spring of 1896, soon after the claims on the head of Sixtymile River, which had hitherto been thought to be in Alaska, were recorded in Canada, and every one thought the commanding officers of the police, being magistrates, would naturally succeed the miners' meeting as the judiciary, a dispute arose between the owner of a claim on one of those creeks and his labourers. The labourers summoned a miners' meeting to settle the difference, and they came. The meeting, after hearing the statements on both sides, dispossessed the owner and put the labourers in charge of the claim. Why they did this was not very clear, there being no detailed report of the meeting. Anyway, the owner of the claim came to Fortymile and laid a complaint before Capt. Constantine, who was Gold Commissioner, and to whom the dispute should have been referred in the first place. After some consideration it was decided to send out a body of ten or twelve policemen, under the command of Lieut. Strickland, to dispossess the labourers and reinstate the owner of the claim. Strickland did this in a considerate manner, which deprived it of much of its sting to the miners. Some time afterwards I met one of those who had been present at the meeting, and asked him why it acted in such a highhanded manner as to deprive a man of his vested rights without a shadow of law to support the act as far as we could see. Further, why it interfered with what it must have known was the prerogative of the magistrates then in the country, whose authority had been acknowledged when record of the claim concerned was made in a Canadian office. He replied, " that the majority of those present felt it was a case in which no process of law as they knew it would do justice." He said " the general impression of the owner was that he was a trickster who did not intend, and could hardly be compelled, under the circumstances, to pay his men. It appeared to them to be a case where a designing, cunning man could hedge himself around by the law, which is supposed to stand for justice, to do an injustice, and as the poor labourers had no money, and felt they could not succeed without it, they appealed to their fellows, who, while knowing that their action was irregular, decided to put themselves on record very emphatically on the side of justice." My friend was a college graduate of more than usual intelligence, possessed of much more than an ordinary knowledge of law, for he had taken a course in it; a man of very high character, a gentleman in the full sense of the word.

He said "with reference to interfering with the offices of the magistrates, that while their act certainly appeared like a wilfully deliberate attempt to do so, they did not look on it in that light, their intention all through the affair being to put themselves on record on the side of fair play and justice as it presented itself to the camp, and if the authorities were appealed to, to submit to their judgment quietly and respectfully. The act of sending out an armed force, as if to compel wrongdoers to retract, was not regarded agreeably at all. All that was necessary was to send them a message that their act was not recognized, and they would have abandoned their position at once, and advised the labourers to try the magistrates for their pay."

Soon after this a Jew tailor and a negro barber in Fortymile had a dispute over accounts. It appeared they had been exchanging commodities for some time without balancing accounts. When one was ready to do so the other was not, and vice versa. At last the Jew determined to bring matters to an issue, and rendered an account which showed a balance of four dollars in his own favour. The barber presented a counter-account, which wiped out the balance, and made one on the other side of one and a half dollars. The Jew, out of respect for what he thought was public opinion, called a miners' meeting, that is, he called a meeting of the residents of Fortymile to be held in a saloon, then kept by a now wealthy Klondiker, to hear the case and decide who owed who, and how much. After due inquiry and deliberate consideration, judgment was entered for the plaintiff, the tailor, in the sum of one dollar and fifty cents, the exact amount the defendant claimed was due to him. As soon as judgment was given, one of the "Solons" present gravely rose and proposed that the tailor be fined in the amount of twenty dollars for calling a meeting to consider such a trifling matter. This was about to be put, and no doubt carried, when an Irishman, who had spent some time in the mining camps of Montana, and had acted as a sheriff's officer, jumped to his feet and shouted, "No! gintlemen, ye can't do that; it's absurd; this poor man has called on ye for jushtice, ye have acknowledged his claim be meetin' and decidin' in his favour, and now ye want to fine him for ashkin' for jushtice; that's nonsensical, ye can't do it." They were awake enough to see the point, and the motion was withdrawn. Had it been carried, the money would have been spent there and then, the reader can guess how. The barber was ordered to pay forthwith, but he rose, and in highly *coloured* language told the assembly that it might or could collectively and individually go to several places not marked on the maps of the Yukon or Alaska. That he would not then, nor at any other time, pay that or any other amount, and if they thought they could get it from him, to try, try! that was all, try!! The police were within hail, and to take him at his word might involve consequences none of them cared about assuming, so the meeting *dissolved*, quietly dissolved into its original elements. It was realized that without power to enforce their decisions miners' meetings were no use. At those meetings, as at every other gathering of curious people, for most of them had no other motive in attending, one or two present led in the talk; it did not follow that they were the best fitted to lead in common sense, but that seldom figures, and sometimes the discussion took a trend no one expected. Early in the spring of 1897 I went over the records of the miners' locations in the townsite, such as it was, of Fortymile, and compared them with the occupants of the ground. The town had organized some years before, elected a registrar to record every new resident as well as

ALASKA COMMERCIAL CO.'S WAREHOUSE, DAWSON, 1897

LAW IN EARLY CAMPS

possible by metes and bounds. The registrars, for there had been several of them, were not surveyors, and the records were so unsatisfactory, compared with the ground, that I deemed it necessary to take them to Ottawa with me, in order that title might properly be issued to the occupants. I advised the registrar that as the records had been given into his custody by a meeting of those interested, he should call another meeting to consider the step I proposed to take. He did so. It happened at that time the registrar was the manager of one of the large trading companies. When he handed me the records, enclosed with them were also the records of the administration of some deceased miners' estates, which I abstracted and handed back to him, they not being related to the business I had in view. When the meeting was called to order, a chairman and secretary were elected. I was then asked to state my purpose in requesting the care of the record book till all the titles were worked out at Ottawa. The records were unanimously voted me for the purpose stated, and the meeting was about to disperse when one of the attendants rose and asked for a hearing, as he had a very important matter to lay before me. When order was restored, he in a most dramatic manner asked "if there were not some other records enclosed with those of the townsite when I got them." I told him there were, and that I had handed them back to the registrar. Now it happened that this man was offended with the registrar, because of some mercantile transactions, and he immediately proceeded to say all manner of reckless things about him with reference to the abstraction of important papers from the records. To my surprise he was taken seriously by a good many present, because they too had trouble with the registrar, as manager of a store, about some accounts. Quite a commotion was being worked up. I rose and asked the chairman if I could say a word or two. Consent was given, order called, and I stated "that to me the situation was a very simple one. The papers in question were no use to me, in the purpose I had in view; I had handed them back to the registrar, who, I had no doubt, had put them carefully away, and if the chairman would nominate a committee of two or three citizens to call on the registrar, and ask for the documents, I had not the least doubt that they would be forthcoming at once." The idea was at once adopted, and in less than five minutes the committee returned with the documents complete and in order. I mention this to show how shallow-brained, unprincipled demagogues can lead better people astray for a time, but then my readers can witness examples of it at almost any public or political meeting. A most glaring example of this occurred at

Fortymile some time before the advent of the Police Magistrates and force. The manager of one of the trading companies had taken with him a woman servant, who was under contract to serve him and his family one year, for which she was to have a suitable wage, board, lodging, and be returned to the coast at the cost of her employer. It was not long till she began to absent herself in the evenings, which was thought peculiar, for the only other woman associate she could have was the mistress of the house, her employer's wife. She was talked to about the irregularity of her conduct, but it seemed to make matters worse. At length her absence in the evenings was so prolonged that it was sometimes morning before she returned, and she refused to give satisfactory explanation of where she was or what she was doing, so the master of the house did the only thing he could do under the circumstances, tell her that if she was not in before a certain hour she would be locked out and dismissed. She disregarded the warning, and it was carried out. She reported to her friends, and a howl of indignation went through the camp. A meeting was called, and with many sobs and tears she told how cruelly she had been used, she was only visiting some friends, etc., etc. A professional man who was in the camp then made a most eloquent appeal on behalf of female misfortune in a

s

frozen, God-forsaken country like that, and so on. The camp was moved to indignation, and it was ordered that the employer be compelled to pay her a full year's wages at the contract rate, to pay her way back to the coast, and to furnish her with sufficient food to last till her departure. This was enforced, but I think some of the parties to the order had to give bond that if ever a proper court came into the country, and the case was tried, and judgment given against the order of the miners' meeting, that the bondmen would have to make restitution to the employer or his company.

It was generally believed afterwards that the orator who was such an ardent advocate for unfortunate womanhood was her partner in misconduct, and that her prolonged stays out at night were in his company. It was also alleged that he benefited personally by the fine imposed on the employer. One of the bondmen, in speaking of it afterwards, told me he was heartily ashamed of the part he had taken in it, but that he, like the others, had been completely hoodwinked by the story the girl told, and judging from the zeal displayed by her advocate, one would never suspect he was her partner in guilt. He told me that "the manager was not over popular in camp, partly personal and partly on account of his company, and he thought that had something to do with the result, but it was mainly the woman's well-acted distress and indignation that brought them round"; it generally does. He for one was willing to contribute at any time his proportion of the sum necessary to recoup the company, but the other bondmen were so scattered, it would be difficult to collect them, even if they were willing to pay. When a proper court was instituted in the country nearly all the principals to the affair had gone from the district, many of them where no process of the court could reach them.

Soon after the Klondike discovery Capt. Constantine, as Gold Commissioner, tried a couple of cases where claim interests were concerned. One was a case of jumping.

When Mr. Fawcett assumed the duties of Gold Commissioner, in June, 1897, there were a good many disputes awaiting his arrival, and during his incumbency—June, 1897, to January, 1899—he certainly earned his small salary. When Judge McGuire came in May, 1898, he assisted Mr. Fawcett all he could, but he was kept very busy with his own court business, and his assistance was not as much as he would have liked.

SEMI-JUDICIAL TRIAL IN THE CAMP

I believe I can claim the honour, if it be one, of trying the first civil case in the Yukon Territory, which arose in this way. A young fellow with not too much of this world's goods had entered the territory to try his fortune. If he were not rich in the precious metals, he was in brass, for his assurance was equal to any occasion. He had been fortunate enough during the winter to secure what is termed a "lay," on a rich bit of ground. A lay is the privilege of working a portion or all of a claim on a percentage of the clean-up. The ground this gentleman got turned out phenomenally rich, and he found himself on the high road to wealth quite unexpectedly. This somewhat increased his self-satisfaction, and he apparently thought the common people did not pay him that respect due to a man of his riches. Among others, he had employed an elderly Frenchman, who, by birth, culture, and education was entitled to all the respect the other fellow thought was his due. This gentleman had fallen on evil days, and had to earn his bread by the sweat of his brow, but he did it like a gentleman. His employer gave him some orders one day in a tone and terms which grated on his sensibilities, and in polished, though caustic, terms he told Newrich what he thought of his style, and protested against a continuation of it in dealing with him. The result was his immediate discharge and a refusal to pay him what was coming to him, until it suited his lord and master, late of the extreme

ICE JAM AT OGILVIE BRIDGE, SHOWING GUGGENHEIM DREDGE AT WORK

democrats, to do so. The amount due the old gentleman, if I recollect aright, was one hundred and fifty-two dollars, and it was all he had in sight after a winter of hard work, and as he was not very well acquainted, his credit was not extensive. He came down from the creek and sought me, I being the one of the officials he was best acquainted with, told me his story, and asked for justice.

Now I had been made a Commissioner of Police in 1887, but what authority that gave me I did not know. I had taken the oath of office before British Columbia's Grand Old Man, Sir Mathew Begbie, and after it was administered he became reminiscent, and told me many stories of his own experience in the early days of the Province, but that, while of some practical value, did not enlighten me much on what a Commissioner of Police was. I knew the law conferred on the office the power of two justices of the peace sitting together, but that was as vague to me as nothing at all, in fact, I knew as little about it as a lawyer, and was willing to admit it. Mr. Fawcett also was a Commissioner of Police, as was Dr. Wills, Surgeon to the Mounted Police, and as both of these gentlemen were in town I reasoned that together we were as strong, legally I mean, as six justices of the peace, and six husky magistrates, I thought, ought to be as strong as a puisne judge, and so we could try the case.

I saw them, and argued that we must not let such a flagrant bit of impertinent injustice go unchallenged. Whether we had authority to try it or not, we could bring this fellow to time, and by so doing create a much-needed and good impression, if we only put on a stiff, bold front. They agreed to sit with me, so I made out a summons to both parties. I had not much experience with summonses, but used all the legal lore I had in getting this one up, and made it look as awesome as possible. I had Fawcett and Wills sign it with me. We then had a policeman serve a copy on both parties; this looked portentous, and created its due impression, for they both promptly attended. I was elected presiding judge, and Robert Craig acted as clerk of court. Each party was sworn. There was no defence, only that the employee had not been duly respectful in his address to his employer, and the employer had withheld payment of the amount due till he could feel the wound to his dignity was healed. With the proper amount of dignity and severity, I hope, I told the employer that the offensive language he complained of was no justification for illegal action on his part, that if he felt very much offended he could have recourse to a magistrate, before whom the case would be tried, and a legal punishment administered. I concluded by ordering him to pay the amount due within twenty-four hours, or further action would be taken. The costs were *nil*. A few hours after I met the defendant on the street, and he stopped me, and in a very saucy manner asked what the consequence would be if he refused to pay the money within the twenty-four hours. I replied, " You will go to the lock-up until you do."

" What! do they put people in jail for debt in Canada ? "

" Not any more than in the United States."

" But they do not do it there."

" Oh, yes, they do; they order a man to pay his debts, and if he does not, he is sent to jail for contempt of court, that is, for not regarding the authority of the law."

" Well, if I refuse to pay in this instance, what will you do ? "

" If you want to learn that, refuse," I replied.

After some reflection he said, " Well, I guess I had better pay up; but if I am a little behind time, you will not be too hard on me."

I replied, " We have already tried the case, we will not do so a second time, and what you ask involves a second trial; if you wanted any consideration of that kind, you should have mentioned it at the court room."

The money was paid early next day, and we gained quite a local reputation as jurists.

A few days after this a man came to see me,

carrying nearly four thousand dollars' worth of gold dust in a deer-skin sack. He told me the dust was the result of a clean-up that five men were interested in. They had made an agreement, but since its execution had swapped, cross swapped, overhead swapped, and subway swapped parts of their interest with each other, till, to use a slang phrase, "they did not know where they were at," and the agreement was interlined and scrawled over till it looked like the manuscript of some of the famous writers, or the draft of a politician's speech. They could not agree as to the division of the clean-up, and the custodian of the dust, learning of the court at Dawson, brought it down and handed it to me, asking that the other parties to the puzzle be summoned to attend, and show cause why they should get any of it. But a summons was not necessary, for the others were close behind him, and seconded his request for a hearing and proper division. This simplified matters, for I did not want to try too many cases, lest I might meet with a reversal. Our first case was disposed of finally, but another might not result so satisfactorily.

The three Commissioners of Police, or six Justices of the Peace, as you may elect, and the Clerk of the Court, as in the previous case, all met the disputants on Saturday afternoon and heard the testimony of each man under oath.

LAW IN EARLY CAMPS

The difficulty was more like an arithmetical puzzle than anything else one could conceive. Between the original agreement, which was deciphered with the aid of the parties, and the evidence, we were seized of all the facts, and the intended facts. Mr. Fawcett was somewhat of a mathematician, but Dr. Wills could not dissect the puzzle as easily as he would have something else. I worked most of Sunday on the thing—there was no Sabbath observance law there then—and *found how old Ann was,* or at least within a year or two of it. I submitted my solution to Fawcett, who accepted it, but Dr. Wills begged to be allowed to jump it as it was. Monday we met, and I solemnly read the judgment of the whole court. Mr. Fawcett, as Gold Commissioner, weighed to each claimant his share of the dust, and all departed satisfied, at least expressed no dissatisfaction.

As far as I know, no more civil cases were tried in Dawson or the territory till the arrival of Justice McGuire.

When Capt. Constantine entered the country, in 1895, he represented the Government generally, being Magistrate, Gold Commissioner, Land Agent, and Collector of Customs. In 1896 Mr. D. W. Davis came in as Collector of Customs. He had for several years been manager for a large trading firm in the north-west of Canada, and had been much in touch with the Department of Customs while in this service. He is credited with telling that while his position and salary were being discussed by the Premier of Canada, Sir Mackenzie Bowell, and himself, that the Premier suggested his taking all the duties he collected for his salary. If this is a fact, and he had accepted, what a salary he would have had in 1897, 1898, 1899, 1900, and 1901! The creeks would have averaged small in comparison. When Mr. Fawcett came in representing the Department of the Interior, in 1897, the service of the territory was pretty well divided, and when Major Walsh came in in 1898, the staff accompanying him, with those there, represented every service, and the country was organized.

DAWSON, 1901

CHAPTER XVI

REFLECTIONS

IT is greatly to the credit of the pioneers of the region that though errors of judgment were committed, as we have seen, no serious crime was ever perpetrated, or attempted, with the exception of the poisoning I have already referred to. We have seen how that attempt was punished, and must admit the sentence was not too harsh. Another crime of a less heinous character was punished by a precisely similar sentence. The story is worth telling. In the fall of 1886 the supply of provisions for the camp on Stewart River was very short. Harper and McQuesten counted heads, and set aside for every man his share of what they had. Many were absent, and probably would not reach the storehouse till well on in the winter, and maybe dead broke then; but that would not count in the distribution. All would share alike, dust or no dust. In those days what might be termed luxuries were not imported in large amounts, being more like holiday fare than everyday food. Among those articles was butter. After the census was taken, the butter, like other articles, was divided equally, and each man, as he came for his share of provisions, got his allowance of butter at the same time. In the camp at that time was a person known as "Missouri Frank," who let it be assumed he was a bad man from somewhere, had notches on his gun, and all the other insignia of the class. Frank was camped about fifteen miles up the Stewart with a partner, not in reputation, but mining. Early in the winter some of their articles of food ran out, among them butter, and Frank hitched himself to his sleigh, and hied him to the post to replenish their stores, never dreaming of a refusal, for he had the dust; and that he thought would be all-prevailing, and only a question of amount. This time he was mistaken. Harper was willing to give him of such things as they had a surplus, which were very few, but of butter there was only the allowance for three or four men who had not yet come in, and that no one else could get at any price. Three or four times the selling price was offered, but without avail. Frank had a reputation to live up to, only he overlooked his surroundings this time. He waited till night, broke into the storehouse, and stole all the butter left took it a mile or two out along the road, hid it, and returned to make a fair start home the next day.

A few days after, one of the delayed parties called for his allotment, when the butter was missed. An examination showed that the door fastenings had been tampered with, and the theft became evident. Harper called a meeting of the miners in camp, laid the facts before them, and speedy action followed. A deputation of three, accoutred for the occasion, was appointed to call on the gentleman from Missouri, and " show him." The deputation was headed by " Bill Love," a Nova Scotian, well known as a " splealer," and wag. I had the pleasure of hearing Bill tell the story, and he told it well. They reached Frank's cabin after the evening meal was over, and immediately upon entering, two of them covered that gentleman with their forty-fives, and the other one the partner. " Hands up!" was the order, and it was bad form to keep them down. Bill then told Frank that they were a little short of butter in the camp, and thinking maybe he had some, they came to borrow a little till next churning time! Frank denied any knowledge of any butter, but Bill told him " he had another think coming, and to hurry up with it, lest his hand got shaky, or his finger cramped, or something like that happened, which might prove unfortunate for some one."

The partner began to see a light dawning, and spoke up, telling Frank to confess, for if he did not, he, the partner, would tell all he knew. Frank would not speak, so the partner told them " that Frank had come home from the camp a few evenings before, with some supplies and a good deal of butter, which he said he had bought from Harper at a high price," in this, lying against Harper and defrauding the partner, for he would have to pay half the amount of the bill. The butter was unearthed, or, to be more precise, unsnowed, and tied on to Frank's sleigh; he was hitched to it, and driven into the camp, hauling the stolen butter, his bedding, and some food with him. Arrived at the camp, he was arraigned before an assembly of all the miners present, the evidence was all put in, the butter identified, and Mr. Frank asked " what he had to say for himself." He would not say anything. It was unanimously voted that he be exiled from camp at least one hundred and fifty miles, and that he never again come near it under penalty of death. He was given his goods, some provisions and ammunition, and escorted out of the camp, up-river, half a day's journey, and watched out of sight.

When I was going down the river with my survey the next summer I saw a man rocking on a bar opposite the mouth of Big Salmon River. I drew in close to shore, and tried to engage him in conversation, but could not get a word out of him. He would not condescend to even look at me. I thought he might be deaf and dumb, but could see that he was not blind. When I reached Fortymile Camp, I learned from Harper and McQuesten who he was. He, I believe, went out up the river that fall, and never was heard from after. This may be considered a severe sentence for such a crime, but the idea appeared to be that he was a bad man, and lest he get the camp into difficulty over a killing, it was deemed best to get rid of him in time. I never heard of even an exchange of shots on the Canadian side of the line. There was one at Circle City, but the good sense of the camp prevailed, and it was stopped, with a severe warning to indulge in no more of it.

At Fortymile there was a challenge issued for a duel through a dispute over a woman. An Englishman and an American quarrelled because the American's squaw accepted too many attentions from the Englishman, so they were to shoot over it. The time was at five in the morning, the place on the ice in front of Fortymile. As the story went, the Englishman appeared at the time and place appointed, armed with a Winchester rifle, and brought with him, in what capacity no one knew, a big Canadian, armed with a double-barrelled shot gun, who remained on top of the bank. The American came along soon after, armed with a large six-shooter. He looked to the front, and there was the Empire; he looked to his left flank, and there, too, was the Empire, one of the five nations furnishing, we may assume, a voluntary contribution to the defence. He was uncertain as to what part that shot-gun would take in the dispute, and the owner was a very sphinx, so he abandoned the field, and fair one. There was peace after, proving that a well-prepared defence makes for good understanding.

The first imprisonment in the territory was made in June, 1897. Some of the police force were in Dawson, under the command of Dr. Wills. They were building quarters and offices for the force. In the town at that time was a log saloon, Joe Ladue's, and several others of canvas or cotton. Two of the latter were large, one of blue stuff, the other of white, and they were known as the Blue and the White Elephant, respectively. It happened one hot day that a more than usual amount of spirit was manifest, a few turned, after the manner of our Scandinavian ancestors, berserker, and if not ferocious, noisy.

That day I was engaged doing something for the miners, and wanted to find another person to get some information. I went into the Blue Elephant looking for him, having been told he was there. In it at the time was a Cornish miner whom I had known for some years. He immediately claimed my attention, and insisted that

BREAKING UP OF THE ICE ON THE YUKON RIVER

I drink with him. I tried quietly to get away, but he was determined that I should have a day with him. There was no use trying to reason with him, so I broke away, and dashed for the door, but he was after me, insisting that I should remain, and began to call me all the vile names in his vocabulary, and he had an extensive one of that character. I tried to quieten him, but he only grew worse, and at last called me a name very common, but to me very offensive, and one I think should justify homicide, yet it is surprising how many men of good standing use it. To knock him down would have been easy in the condition he was in, but I restrained myself, and called on a policeman, who had been listening to him for some time, to take him away and put him in the lock-up. There was one building, the walls of which were complete, but there was no roof on it yet, so a jail was improvised out of that, and the prisoner was shut in. A little while after this I heard an uproar in a saloon not far away. I went over, and found that a white man and his Indian woman were having a stand-up fight. The woman's mouth was bleeding, and the man had a cut on his cheek, where she had landed on him. I believe she was getting the best of it, but I stepped between them and stopped it, apparently much to the dissatisfaction of the woman. I then addressed a few remarks to the saloon keeper, and stepped out and called a police-

T

man, and directed him to take them both to the lock-up.

Soon after this, the Irishman whom I have mentioned in connection with the miners' meeting, held to adjust the difference of account between the Jew tailor and the negro barber, under the influence of various motives—some sentimental, some physical, and some spirituous—grew eloquent and noisy, principally the latter, on the rights of his fellow citizens who had just been ignominiously committed to prison for simply enjoying their undoubted privileges. For awhile it was amusing, but all amusements soon pall, and this not only palled, but became offensive to all who had to listen, and so Dr. Wills, now that we had a lock-up, ordered his arrest and incarceration. It was a terrible blow, for, like many other would-be apostles of liberty, he found that amusement may cause more applause than conviction, and no one rushed to his rescue. All four culprits had to remain in the roofless prison all night, and the contemplation of the starless sky must have brought wisdom, for in the morning all except the Irishman were penitent, acknowledged their error, and were willing to promise anything to obtain their liberty. They all promised to leave town for their claims at once, if let go, and they did.

The old miner wept, and declared he had been a miner for more than forty years, and had never been in jail before. He had come into town for a pound of tea, and as soon as he was at liberty he went to a store and bought it. A bystander, as he was getting the tea, remarked, " Have a drink, Bob," and Bob turned on him in wrath, said some things, and fled for the hills as though running for his life. The man and his Indian woman did not wait for anything, but took over the hills, as though the town were plague-infested. But the Irishman —well, he was different—he would not even leave his prison. As he was the Doctor's prisoner I let the Doctor deal with him, and he harangued that gentleman for nearly half an hour, dilating on all the damages he was going to claim from the British Government, or the Canadian Government, or any Government he could reach, for false imprisonment, and he was going to rot in the vile dungeon rather than damage his prospects by leaving even for a moment. " Tin thousand—t-i-n t-h-o-u-s-a-n-d dollars — d'ye hear, is the very laste cint I'll take." The Doctor retired, leaving him to his reflections. After a little more sleep, he consented, as the workmen wanted the premises, to leave under protest. Down town he found an unaccountable apathy. No one seemed interested in his case, unless manifest amusement is interest ; so after wasting some eloquence on the desert air, he betook himself to his camp. The action for damages never was brought, and as the poor fellow died in the Philippine Islands a few years ago, there will be no action.

We were congratulated by a good many for ridding the town of a nuisance.

The first prisoner extradited from Yukon Territory was arrested in Dawson early in July, 1897. The charge against him was murder, committed in the State of Iowa, U.S.A., in the early spring of that year. The victim was a well-known old farmer, who had acted as parent, guide, and friend to the murderer; and the motive was to secure, through the wife of the murderer, life insurance to the amount of 30,000 dollars on his own life. The old man was decoyed to his foster son's office late in the night, shot to death, and the premises then fired to conceal the crime and to convey the impression that the murderer himself had been burned to death. The fire, though it charred the body did not destroy every means of identification, and after a few days' investigation, it was positively recognized as that of the old farmer, by clue it is unnecessary here to state. Application had been made for the insurance money, but the identification of the body stopped payment, and the insurance company placed the tracing of the murderer in the hands of a Chicago detective, named Perrin. At the investigation it was established that the body had been shot through the heart, and the murderer's financial circumstances revealed the motive for the crime. After a careful examination of the premises, and inquiry into everything that would aid in the trace, the detective concluded that the criminal would make for the Klondike, the name being then familiar, where, if he reached it, he would seek to lose his identity. As this place is in Canada, extradition papers would be necessary were he found there, and the detective went to Ottawa, the seat of government in Canada, laid his facts before the Minister of Justice, and in two days everything necessary to deport the criminal, should he be found in the Yukon region, was completed. The detective returned to the scene of the crime, gathered what additional information he could, part of it being a detailed description of the suspect and a small photograph of him, taken many years before. He hurried to Seattle, the United States northwestern port for the Klondike, sought for clues, one of which led him back to Philadelphia, there to find he was after the wrong man. Back to Seattle he rushed, sought for, and found evidence of a man answering the description having gone north on one of the Skagway-bound steamers.

Even at that early date, June, 1897, the rush was wild, and hardly a rod of the dreary twenty-three miles over Dyea Pass but showed signs of some eager slave to the universal passion. Men and women, good and bad, adventurers and adventuresses, saints and sinners, simple and wise, cunning and guileless, strong and weak, healthy and sickly, rich and poor, young and old, clothed and ragged, women in their ordinary dress, women in part male and part female attire, and many entirely in male clothing—all mad with a common madness, nearly all wise in council for the common weal, many, many brutes in action for their own. Some sinking to lower than bestial shamelessness in conduct and association, and strangely, too, I was almost saying, but only consistently after all, some of the most degraded, degraded beneath decent designation, posed in Dawson as immaculate, and were the greatest censors of the government and public officials.

Straggling along the route from tide water to the summit, fifteen miles away and two-thirds of a mile above it, and from the summit to Lake Lyndeman, eight miles farther, and a fourth of a mile below it, was this motley crowd of many tongues and nations, in which Detective Perrin sought his man, but in vain; for the indifference to attire and cleanliness, begotten of such a rude life and its surroundings, works wonderful changes in the personal appearance of most men. Down the river Perrin continued the almost hopeless search. Every boat was searched, and its occupants scrutinized for future reference, for it might prove that some one else " wanted " would be sighted, but no face reminded him of the photograph he had or recalled the figure he had in mind.

Arrived at Dawson, its myriads of tents and their ever-flitting occupants seemed like the proverbial haystack in which he had to search for his needle. Almost hopeless, he began a systematic watch, conducted so as to occasion as little notice as possible. At last a faint suspicion arose. One tent was noted, which contained three men, only two of whom moved about during the day, the other only momentarily showing himself in the daylight hours, being always confined to the tent, ostensibly by the cooking necessary for the party. After midnight, with hat well pulled down and lowered head, he would take a quiet stroll in the unfrequented parts of the town. It was difficult to get a good look at his features, even if it were daylight all the time, and to act too boldly might lose him altogether, for any one could be lost in a moment in that land of mountain and moor.

Night after night, Perrin watched the suspect's jaunts, until something in his eyes reminded him of the eyes in the photograph, and gradually, like the lineaments in a puzzle picture, the face in the photograph was revealed through the heavy beard and moustache the suspect now wore. He recognized in him also a dirt-begrimed, ragged, taciturn man he had noticed in the pass several times, but now, as he was clean and dressed, one could see what his features resembled.

Soon suspicion became conviction, and Perrin applied to Capt. Constantine, then the only peace official in the territory, for the arrest and deportation of the suspect. The extradition papers were found in order, and the commanding officer had the man arrested. The resemblance to the photograph and description was found satisfactory, which together with his suspicious conduct while in Dawson, made good cause for his extradition, and he was placed in charge of the detective for that purpose.

The prisoner naturally denied all knowledge of the case, declaring he hailed from another part of the country, and gave a false name, J. L. Smith, under which name he had been travelling. A stalwart policeman, whose term of service was nearly expired, was allowed to accompany the detective to assist in looking after the prisoner. On the morning of July 14th, they left Dawson on the river steamer *John J. Healey*, for St. Michael, the Bering Sea port of entry for Yukon, situated on an island of the same name on the easterly shore of Norton Sound, about seventy miles north-east of the mouth of the Yukon River.

I went from Cudahy to St. Michael with them, and heard the story as I have related it, from the lips of Perrin.

LOOKING SOUTH FROM POINT ON THE 141ST MERIDIAN, 1896

At the mouth of the river we ran, with a falling tide, on to a muck bar, and were nearly twenty-four hours there. In windy weather river steamers cannot make the run from the mouth of the river to St. Michael, Norton Sound becoming too rough for such frail craft to live in. When we got clear of the bar and mouth of the river, a north-west wind arose, and we had to put out two anchors, and lie for forty-eight hours in water so shallow that at low tide the boat often bumped the mud bottom, and we drew only two and a half feet, yet we were more than half a mile from shore.

The wind was so fierce that at times we expected the light cabins to be blown off, and so cold that we spent most of the time in the saloon or dining-room, it serving both purposes, where a brisk fire was kept going in a large stove, notwithstanding that it was July.

At noon on Sunday, July 25th, we reached St. Michael, where we all had to await an outward-bound steamer for several weeks. Here quarters for the prisoner and guards were found in the North American Transportation and Trading Company's premises at Fort "Get There," as it was then called.

During the wait, Perrin requested me to photograph the prisoner, first with beard on, after which he would be shaved and another photograph taken. As the pictures were intended for use in court when the trial was on, I took Perrin into the dark room, where I loaded a holder with two plates, on each of which I marked with a soft pencil the date and my initials. I then requested the detective to put on his initials, the date, and any other marks of identification he thought necessary.

I exposed both plates on the prisoner with the detective sitting beside him. As my camera was not a portrait one, and the exposure was made in an ordinary room, the pictures cannot be called a great success, though the likeness to each man is very fair. One of the plates I developed, and made some prints from, some of which were given to Perrin. Both the developed and undeveloped plates were then carefully packed. After the prisoner was shaved, the photographing was repeated as above, then the four plates were placed in a waterproof box, and the detective took them with him to Iowa, where the other two were developed, and prints from all four were used in the court.

Of the copies retained, I have lost or mislaid all but one. At the time I made the prints I had no way of toning my work, and the proof—it is nothing more—was simply carefully fixed, so its tone is not quite orthodox. I have hundreds of times shown the picture to people, remarking as I did so, " Here is a picture of a cruel murderer and the detective who followed him nine thousand miles to arrest him. Now, which is the murderer?" Very seldom is the right one chosen.

When more than two weeks at St. Michael had passed, Perrin had an opportunity to leave with his prisoner for Iowa. Not long after his arrival there, the prisoner was put on trial and convicted; but some of the jurors being opposed to capital punishment, brought in a verdict of murder in the second degree, which does not necessitate the death sentence. In consequence the murderer got off with only twenty years' imprisonment.

As arranged between us, the detective wrote me a synopsis of the trial, and sent me papers containing a full report of it.

This has brought the record down to the organization of the territory, and the advent of official supervision of every department of governmental administration, and that was as far as I intended to go with this record. Since that time, official records relate all that has been done; before that, the recollections of a few individuals with a few records, mostly unofficial, were all that could be looked to for authentic information. I have tried to give the gist of all this that came within my ken to the best of my judgment and ability.

Some day, when events justify it, the history of the country will be written fully from that date, but there is hardly enough of great note since the organization to justify it yet.

The camp, in its early days, was often on the verge of starvation. This was particularly so in the winter of 1885-6, and, again, especially so in the winter and spring of 1896-7; but it was found there was plenty for all, though not much to spare.

The following anecdote, told me by Long John, whom the reader will recollect in connection with the attempt to reach Stewart River from Fortymile by steamer in the fall of 1887, will illustrate how close the camp was to actual want in the spring of that year.

"Whin I raked tigether all me provisions ti start for the new digging at Fortymile, I found I had d——n little. I got ready ti lave about the middle o' March, and down to Fortymile was a long haul, a hundred an' twinty mile we called it. I had only wan dog ti help me, an' nothing for that one ti ate barrin' the dishwashin's, which id be d——d thin on the way down. Well, I found I was purty short iv ivrythin', but more so iv flour than anythin' else. I shuck out all me old sacks, and turned thim inside out, an' thin dusted thim. Whin I got through I had about forty pounds of purty d——d dirty luckin' stuff, ye could call it flour if ye wanted ti, but ye needn't if ye didn't want ti. The rest iv me stuff was purty much the same. Altogether I had about a month's provisions, an' how I was going to live on it till the first boat got up, maybe in July, maybe in August, was more than I could tell, unless I tuck ti the woods, an' thin we had d——d little ammunition. I knew I'd waste a lot iv me flour, bad as it was, be mixing it every time I'd bake, so ti save as much as possible, I mixed it all with bakin' powder, an' thin put enough water in it to make a nice batter, an' whin the whole lot was well mixed, I put it outside ti' freeze. When I wanted bread I'd rowl it up agin the fire, and whin it was purty black on that side I'd knock off the cooked part, an' ate it. This saved me a lot of trouble while on the way down the river, for it was d——d cowld, I dunno how cowld it was, for me mercury was solid, an' the painkiller was purty thick, so it must a been below forty. Well, sir, one mornin' I got up ti get me bread ready, an' me ball iv flour was gone. I lucked and lucked, but the divil a sign iv it could I see. I lucked at me dog, but he, poor divil, lucked as hungry as iver, an' as innocent as a lamb. I was stumped! an' couldn't make head nor tail iv it, but there I was without me flour. I lucked around, gettin' farther from camp all the time, till I saw signs on the ice like what somethin' bein' rowled along would make, an' I followed it clane across the river, and there, up agin the bank where he couldn't rowl it any farther, was me ball iv flour, an' it was a sight, shure! The poor divil iv a dog had scratched it wid his paws, an' gnawed it wid his teeth, tryin' ti get somethin' off it, till it was scratched all over. I tuck it back ti the fire, and the dog lucked the guiltiest thing ye ever saw, but I hadn't the heart ti touch him, poor divil, he was starvin', for I had nothin' but bacon rind ti give ti him, and not much iv that. I lucked at me ball iv flour for a long time, thinkin' whether I'd cut off all the outside where it was scratched an' licked, but I couldn't afford to waste it. It was d——d hard, but I had ti cook it an' ate it."

An incident occurred in the spring of 1896 that illustrates a phase of human nature, called by various names, and discussed from various standpoints, which I will let the reader view as he likes, and analyse as he pleases. A resident of Fortymile, not having much to do, and money, or dust, being scarce with him, thought he would distil some " hootch," the name given a brand of whisky distilled from the fermentation of flour and molasses, or from anything else that would ferment, but those articles were most frequently used.

I have seen the Indians on the coast making it, using for the condensing worm the long stem of a species of seaweed very common in the north. While the distillation is going on, they sit watching the liquor drop from the worm, and drink it as fast as a mouthful gathers.

Our friend made his worm out of tin or iron pipes as he found them most readily. When he had some eight or ten gallons of the liquor, he called on Capt. Constantine to learn what to do to be safe in trafficking in the stuff. The Captain told him he had no control over him disposing of it, but he would have to collect from him the excise duty on it. Now he might have said nothing about what he was doing, and disposed of it quietly, and this excise was a shock to his puny pocket. However, he paid, and arranged his plan of operation, which was to take it to the best paying creeks and sell it either retail or wholesale as suited the convenience of his customers. The miners on the two leading creeks, Miller and Glacier, learning, as he intended they should, of his intentions, held a meeting, and resolved: That in the event of any party or parties coming to their creeks with intoxicating liquors to sell, they would seize the liquor, spill it, and send the party or parties whence they came with a warning. Our distiller heard of this, but smiled, and thought, "Well, we'll see."

Nothing daunted, he loaded his sled with his bed, some provisions, and the precious liquor, and hauled the lot to a vacant cabin convenient to the mouths of both creeks, where he took up his abode. The miners knew he had started, ostensibly, for their creeks, and when he was some time overdue, became anxious about him. At last his whereabouts was learned, and their indignation was increased, if that were possible. But indignation, like other volatile things, is evanescent, and as nature abhors a vacuum, one of them, on the following afternoon, took down his rifle, and proclaimed his intention of going out to look for a caribou; he was *tired of eating bacon*, and yearned for a bit of *fresh meat*. He returned next morning, weary and tired from his hunt; he had not seen any caribou, but *had seen* good signs, and might take another look around before long. That evening another hunter went out to look up the signs, and see whether it might not be the animals' spring migration. It was! When the caribou were all secured and the keg empty, the distiller returned to town with a well-filled "poke," the price of numerous caribou killed out of season. When all the fresh meat in camp was disposed of, another meeting was called, and more stringent resolutions passed against whisky-sellers, death, I think, being one of the penalties to be inflicted on the next transgressor; but the spring migration had carried the caribou down to town by the time another keg was ready.

The making of hootch was never much resorted to in the territory—to its credit be it said. One of the boys in 1889, I think it was, brewed, not "a peck o' maut," but something else, not quite so palatable, but maybe equally

LOOKING UP TAKU PASS NEAR SUMMIT, 1895

potent, and invited, like " Willie," some of his " frien's " to come and " prie." Just to add to the amusement a game of poker was begun ; a dispute arose, which ended in a quarrel in which knives were brandished. Good sense, however, prevailed, and when sobriety returned, it was agreed that never again would any of that gathering encourage hootch-making.

CHAPTER XVII

SOCIAL CUSTOMS

IT can readily be perceived that, in such a cosmopolitan community, anything like common customs or social habits would be most conspicuous by their absence. One feature of human nature which is as wide as humanity itself prevailed there just as it does everywhere else, and under every adverse condition of the country, that is the fun-making feature, which has been sometimes called *the* human attribute in contradistinction to the purely animal.

As we have seen in the earlier years of the river's history, no mining was done in winter, during which the miners, as a rule, settled around the supply posts, and if we may judge from the stories told, endeavoured in every way they could devise to make up for the loneliness of their isolation in small hard-worked groups during the summer. Playing practical jokes on one another, both individually and collectively, was a source of much amusement; but the organization of story-telling clubs appears to have been one of, if not *the* principal feature of winter diversion.

Consequently, the tales related grew, from something more then natural and probable proportions, to very prominent Münchhausen dimensions.

In the fall of 1887-8, a camp of seven or eight miners was formed on an island in the Yukon, a mile or two above Fortymile. This group developed such inventive powers in story-telling that the island was named " Liars' Island," and the denizens, the " Forty Liars," it being held that though only seven or eight in number, they were equal in talent to the forty liars in story. The miners evidently had in mind liars instead of thieves. This club held regular meetings which as many outsiders attended as room could be found for in the small cabin club-room. Whether a programme and subject for succeeding meetings was given out at the close of the preceding ones, I cannot say; but the stories, generally, were confined for the evening to one subject, and each story might be commented on, or reflected on without offence. The nature of the stories is already apparent; the value of them as efforts will appear from these samples. The sagacity of animals appears to have been the subject for the evening, and one narrator told of a tame beaver an uncle of his possessed, which happened one night to have been shut in the parlour, where it had been entertaining some visitors during the evening with its wonderful intelligence. In the night a water-pipe which ran along the wall of the room burst, and soon the water was flooding the apartment. The beaver, true to its instinct, at once began to dam the flood, cutting up and using for that purpose all the furniture in the room, the piano included; using the chairs and sofa coverings and stuffing, and the carpet on the floor in place of the mud found in its native haunts to fill the interstices in the dam, and make it watertight. In the morning, when the household arose, they found the animal " busy as a beaver," building up the dam to hold the water in one part of the room. It had cut down the door of the room and added it to the dam, and was busy on the hall furniture when they relieved it. A listener sagely remarked that the feat only went to prove what he had known since childhood, that the beaver was, it might be said, superhuman in its intelligence and capacity for work. He recalled some memories of a beaver that belonged to his grandfather, with which as a child he often played. His grandfather kept a general store, and it happened one evening that the beaver got into the basement where the syrup, sugar, and other bulky commodities were kept. Now this particular evening was unusually cold; some syrup was asked for, an attendant went to the hogshead containing it, opened the spigot, placed the measure under it, and waited for the cold, thickened liquid to fill it.

This took so long that the customer became impatient, and his annoying importunity made the clerk forget to close the spigot. The beaver soon found the flowing stream, realized that a serious loss would result if some preservative measure were not at once taken; so laid itself on its back with its open mouth under the spigot, and swallowed the precious stuff as fast as it descended. In the morning it was found at its post still trying to hold the syrup as it flowed out, though its capacity was being strained to the breaking-point, the hogshead being about two-thirds empty, having been almost full at the start. The narrator of the "dam" story remarked, "That ain't a natural story by a *dam site*." "Well," was the prompt response, "haven't I the same *site* to tell a *dam* good story that you have?"

Another evening the subject of contest appeared to have been the quantity, or amount, of camp supplies they had seen at any one time. One of the club, named Steele, was famous as a "spealer." He gravely told of having seen in his experience in the mining camps in British Columbia, many years before, ONE HUNDRED AND THIRTY-NINE CORDS OF BACON piled on the bank of the North Thompson River. Some one said, "Ah! come now, Steele, take off a cord or two"; "Not a G—d d—n rind," was the instant and emphatic reply. When the reader reflects that a cord is eight feet long, four wide, and four high, he can form some idea of the size of the pile. As to why Steele employed such unfamiliar terms of bulk, each may decide for himself, but it is evident a cord of bacon is much more original as a definition than a ton, and leaves it to be worked out just how much was there.

In a community where so many communistic ideas prevail, it is needless to say class distinctions were prohibited, and any one who tried to raise them was not only despised, but was unmistakably shown that he was. The manager of one of the big trading companies, who assumed office a short time before the Klondike discovery, came in with rather European ideas as to the importance of his position. He had commercial jurisdiction over all the Yukon valley and, the miners thought, put on airs co-extensive with it. He really was not a bad fellow, and by those with whom he was acquainted was generally highly esteemed. His exclusiveness, however, did not go down with the miners, and they set about conferring on him a title which they imagined would accord with his own ideas of his importance. At first, the " Duke of St. Michael " was suggested, but that was soon rejected as too local; St. Michael was only a trading-post, so the " Prince of Alaska " was tried for a while, but that was not considered quite comprehensive enough; it was generally believed the gentleman considered himself infallible, so some one suggested the " Pope," which stuck.

It is hardly necessary to say that religious feeling or prejudice, one way or the other, had nothing to do with the bestowal of this title. In such cosmopolitan gatherings, where religious observances or exercises are very little practised, religious sentiments and prejudices soon become dulled, and are often discussed, in not too orthodox style. For myself, I might say I have no feeling, and intend no disrespect to any denomination in telling this story; to me it is a story : nothing more or less.

It happened that among the incomers about this time was a rather elderly woman, with her husband ; advisedly I have placed her first. She had lived a fairly long frontier life, which, added to her natural characteristics, gave her a widely known and respected facility for expressing her feelings in sharp, crisp, frontier style. The husband had staked a Klondike claim in the first days of the rush. Means they had not too much of, so to help out, the wife took in laundry work, and in her clientele was the family of the distinguished gentleman referred to. When the proper season enabled work on the claim to be done, messages began to come in from the husband, giving higher and higher values to the pans as the work progressed. Visions of prospective wealth and ease appear to have produced negligence in the laundry, but as there was no competition there could be no choice, and the slighted work was borne to the limit of patience. When, one day, our lofty friend returned a parcel of botched garments by the hands of a messenger, with a haughty, emphatic order, " to do the clothes in a proper manner, and return them in a proper condition ! " the messenger delivered the order word for word and tone for tone. The wife was busy over the wash-tub at the time, but straightened up, placed her arms akimbo, and with an emphasizing nod of the head to every word, said, " Tell the Pope to go plumb to h—l; Jack's getting forty dollars to the pan now."

The story got out, and the old lady, as she was styled, was, figuratively speaking, heartily slapped on the back, and unanimously commended as a good fellow. Had Jack's pans not yielded plentifully, I verily believe a subscription would have been taken up for them, the story was so much enjoyed and applauded.

The worthy pair accumulated from numerous forty-dollar pans a fortune that would have seemed fabulous to them a year before that time, and are now living in retired ease in a lovely home.

CHAPTER XVIII

HOME

A FITTING conclusion to this, as to every enterprise or labour, is "Home"; home, the miner's cabin, what he built it of, and how he built it. What he built it of was always what he could find adjacent to the site he chose, and as the prevailing timber of the region is spruce and poplar, the walls and roof consisted of logs of those trees, of such size and length as the party of one or more who were to house themselves in it could conveniently handle. The roof consisted of small poles laid from ridge-pole to the wall on either side; on this series of beams, as they might be termed, was put a layer of the moss found so abundantly in the country, of a depth of about a foot; on this was placed about an equal thickness of the clay of the place. This made a close, warm roof, and in summer-time, unless the rain fell unusually heavy, it was dry too.

After the size of the building had been decided on, a space somewhat larger in extent was cleared of the surface moss, leaves, and sticks; on this the two first logs were laid parallel to each other, the ends saddled to receive the notched ends of the next pair of logs to be laid on the saddles prepared for them. The ends of the last pair were then saddled as with the first pair, and so on, till the height of the walls was reached. On the ends of the building walls sloped logs were laid, and fastened to those below them by wedges or pins, as proved most convenient to the builder; on the apex of this slope was laid the ridge-beam or beams, there being sometimes two, the height of which above the side-walls determined the slope of the roof. In the walls, as they rose, were left openings for the door and window, or windows, which were dressed to measure, and squared after the walls were finished. The door was made of slabs; it might be split from suitable logs, or, if possible, whip-sawed from the same. Very often the door was mounted on wooden pin-hinges, made on the spot, as household hardware was not much dealt in in the earlier years of the territorial settlements. Glass was often scarce, and other means of admitting light through the windows had to be substituted. Sometimes untanned deer-hide, from which the hair had been removed, was used; this was translucent to a limited degree, but not by any means transparent. Sometimes a bit of white cotton canvas was used, and sometimes empty white glass bottles or pickle jars were placed on end on the window-sill, and the interstices between

INTERIOR OF AUTHOR'S CAMP NEAR BOUNDARY, 1895

them stuffed with moss. Whatever method was used to admit light, it made but little difference in the result; for the intense frosts so soon covered the surface of the media, that light was practically shut out; indeed, in the long winter nights, about twenty hours out of the twenty-four windows were of very little use anyway, and in the summer months the miner only used his cabin to sleep in, and he invited darkness rather than light.

The walls, door, and windows finished, the spaces between the logs, and every other space visible, was chinked, or stuffed, with moss, driven in tight by suitably shaped sticks. The furniture consisted of stools, the seats of which were hewn, or sawed, from blocks of trees, and were supported by three or four legs. Tables and beds were laid on small beams, one end of which was driven between two of the wall logs, and the other supported by uprights driven into the ground. On the bed, beams were laid parallel with the wall, small poles, and on these grass, if it could be got, and where it could not, the smaller branches of the spruce tree; on this mattress was spread the blankets and other covering. Sleep on this primitive bed was as sound as that enjoyed anywhere, and the food eaten off the rough, uncovered table tasted as well as if laid on the finest mahogany. Table-ware consisted of tin plates, tin cups, and the cheapest and strongest of spoons, knives and forks. Cooking was mostly done in frying-pans, called spiders, and bake-kettles, or dutch-ovens, a cast-iron pot, with a close-fitting top of the same metal. These last were made in nests enclosed in one another for convenience of packing.

Stoves were almost unknown at first, and fire-places of rock were built in the cabin; as an opening in the top to let the smoke escape was prohibited on account of the low temperatures, these fire-places had to be closed on top, and at the rear end continued to the roof in a chimney. Sometimes, where suitable rock and good clay could be found, these fire-places were rather artistic in form and finish, and certainly very comfortable, for the mass of rock, once heated, retained the heat a long time. The size of the cabin would shock a hygienist, as no account of air-space was taken in the design, the first consideration being warmth. It was not an uncommon thing for a cabin, say sixteen feet by eighteen, to house four or more men. My winter quarters at the boundary for seven men was twenty-two feet square inside, and was thought palatial in dimension; it certainly was in comfort, being well heated by a rock stove three feet wide, three high, and eight long; the rear end, three feet square, continued in a chimney to the roof. All this mass of rock was bound together by an excellent clay we found near.

Ventilation was secured by two ventilators, one long one bringing the cold fresh air down in rear of the chimney, which heated it, and the other one carried the heated foul air out at the other end of the building. I never spent a more comfortable winter in my life than in that house.

APPENDIX

BY DR. ALFRED THOMPSON, M.P.

THE foregoing reminiscences by Mr. William Ogilvie contain probably the most complete of the several authentic accounts now extant of the discovering, mapping, and settlement of " The Empire's Furthest North." A surveyor and mathematician by training and inclination, he at the same time possessed, to a rare degree, the qualities which go to make up an exceptionally interesting raconteur. Thus, in the exact detailing of the events which developed the Yukon for Canada and the Empire, he does not lose sight of any of the romance thereof. An illuminating character sketch, a graphic story or some gem of colloquialism, aid materially in imparting to the reader the true atmosphere. After all, these men who opened up the North, while of an heroic mould, were of our own flesh and blood. And nowhere does Mr. Ogilvie fall into the error of regarding the age of heroism as past. What they did was big. That which they added to the known world was immense. But with a little story or two he brings his heroes out of the clouds down to our own level ; and we grasp them and understand them in a way quite impossible from the reading of much more pretentious works than this book of reminiscences of Mr. William Ogilvie.

With a modesty which is characteristic, the author

APPENDIX

lays down his pen at the very point in the history of Yukon where most men in the same position would have taken it up to write. Mr. Ogilvie was practically the first Governor of that territory. His predecessor, Major Walsh, held the position but a few months, and the task of laying the beginnings of a Government was left to Mr. Ogilvie. It was under his hand that a vast wilderness in the inaccessible North became a populous territory in a single year. Distracted and torn with eagerness to possess some of the marvellous flow of gold of which the world was then talking, this army of adventurers had to be controlled. Laws had to be created for the administration of the country, and the conditions were without precedent. Ninety per cent of the people were aliens, and a hundred per cent were individualistic to a remarkable degree. There were neither mails nor telegraphs, neither roads nor bridges. The only existent mining regulations were completely inadequate. An army of officials had to be created out of the most unpromising material, from men mostly half mad from the craze for sudden wealth. Every man spoke and thought for himself. The source of all authority was at Ottawa, four thousand miles away, requiring months in which to refer a single question or to get a solitary ruling. Meanwhile the need was for instant legislation—rulings on the moment, and it was into this seething whirl of eagerness, discontent, greed, and prodigality Mr. Ogilvie was cast as Governor or Commissioner in the summer of 1896. An entire system had to be created. Advisers were plenty, for every man in the country considered himself quite capable of suggesting a solution of every problem. But in the multitude of counsel there was no wisdom, since very few agreed. There was no precedent. Mr. Ogilvie's powers as Commissioner were greater in many respects than the powers of a governor elsewhere, but the Federal Government of Ottawa still held the reins. All expenses were on a scale of at least four to one—wages four times what they were anywhere else in Canada ; and costs of supplies of all kinds the same. And, while fabulously rich claims were pouring out gold in disconcerting amounts, the value of most of the ground was quite normal. The Federal authorities at Ottawa were being advised by the Press and public men to see to it that a share of Klondike's great wealth found its way into the public coffers. Thus, for a term, there was the inclination to say " No " to expensive requisitions and to insist upon large taxes, which could have easily been paid by certain of the fabulously rich claims I have mentioned, but which spelled ruin for many of the miners in the country.

Mr. Ogilvie did wonderful things in the situation I have described. The best men available at that time were drafted into the service. Mining regulations for mining were devised. Civil courts and schools were established. Mails were contracted for. Voluminous information was dispatched. The criminal administration became the model of the world. Multitudinous public grievances, many of them most real and acutely serious, were abated one by one. Order was gradually evolved out of chaos. Departments were organized and authority segregated. The whole work was colossal and epochal, and in his book Mr. Ogilvie modestly lays it all aside with the naive suggestion that, from where he leaves off in his writings, the rest may easily be taken up from the official records. He only concerns himself with that which, else, might have been lost for ever.

Since the closing of Mr. Ogilvie's narrative much has

APPENDIX 305

happened. Yukon is down now to a business basis in every way. The government of the country has been largely delegated to its wholly elective council of ten representatives, who meet as a little Parliament, elect a speaker, impose local taxes, and arrange for disbursements. With such a local body, immediately responsive to every public wish and movement, one may easily forget the difficulties besetting Yukon's first legislator.

In a material way the changes are still greater. The fabulously rich claims of the early days have been worked out, reworked by improved methods, and with much other hand have fallen into the hands of companies able, by the use of large capital and improved methods, to extract still further amounts of gold therefrom. The developments which Mr. Ogilvie in his book so clearly foresees have all come about. To-day (1913) we have a fleet of thirteen great dredges digging gold in the vicinity of Dawson. These machines are all driven by electricity and run night and day during the working season. Great hydraulic mines are working on many of the hills on Bonanza and Hunker creeks, and plans and works are under-way for repeating this over the Divide in the Indian River watershed. The water to work the present hydraulics is brought by a great ditch, with siphons and flumes of steel and wood, for seventy-two miles over a range of mountains, and is perhaps the longest in the world constructed for that purpose.

Copper is to-day being successfully mined in the vicinity of White Horse. Immense deposits of copper ore have been discovered in the vicinity of White River, and only await transportation to make them most valuable. Coal exists in large quantities in the territory, as is demonstrated by the Geological Survey Department of

Canada. Grazing is just beginning, and will in all probability develop into a thriving industry in the south-east portion of the territory, where horses can live out all winter and find fodder in the succulent grasses indigenous to that section.

The future of this vast region is full of hope, as it is generously endowed. The resources are rich and varied and only await the pick of the prospector, the plough of the farmer, and the advent of the horse and cattle rancher to make it what one day it will truly be—Canada's great Reserve.

GOLD

HISTORICAL AND ECONOMIC ASPECTS

An Arno Press Collection

[Bonus, Petrus of Ferrara]. The New Pearl of Great Price. 1894

Emmons, William Harvey. Gold Deposits of the World: With a Section on Prospecting. 1937

Father Coughlin on Money and Gold: Three Pamphlets. 1974

Gold and Silver in the Presidential Campaign of 1896. 1974

Gold Mining Company Prospectuses. 1974

Hammond, John Hays. The Autobiography of John Hays Hammond. 1935. 2 volumes in one

Johnson, Obed Simon. A Study of Chinese Alchemy. 1928

Letcher, Owen. The Gold Mines of Southern Africa. 1936

Nesbitt, L[ewis] M[ariano]. Gold Fever. 1936

Ogilvie, William. Early Days on the Yukon and the Story of its Gold Finds. 1913

[Preshaw, G. O.]. Banking Under Difficulties or Life on the Goldfields of Victoria, New South Wales & New Zealand. By a Bank Official. 1888

Rickard, T[homas] A[rthur]. Man and Metals. 1932. 2 volumes in one

Russell, Henry B. International Monetary Conferences. 1898

Seyd, Ernest. **Bullion and Foreign Exchanges Theoretically and Practically Considered.** 1868

Speculation in Gold and Silver Mining Stocks. 1974

Taylor, F. Sherwood. **The Alchemists:** Founders of Modern Chemistry. 1949

United States Congress. House of Representatives. Committee on Banking and Currency. **Gold Panic Investigation.** 41st Congress, 2d Session, House Report No. 31. 1870

Weaver, James B. **A Call to Action.** 1892

COLORADO MOUNTAIN COLLEGE
LRC--WEST CAMPUS
Glenwood Springs, Colo 81601